SMITHSONIAN CONTRIBUTIONS TO ANTHROPOLOGY

NUMBER 13

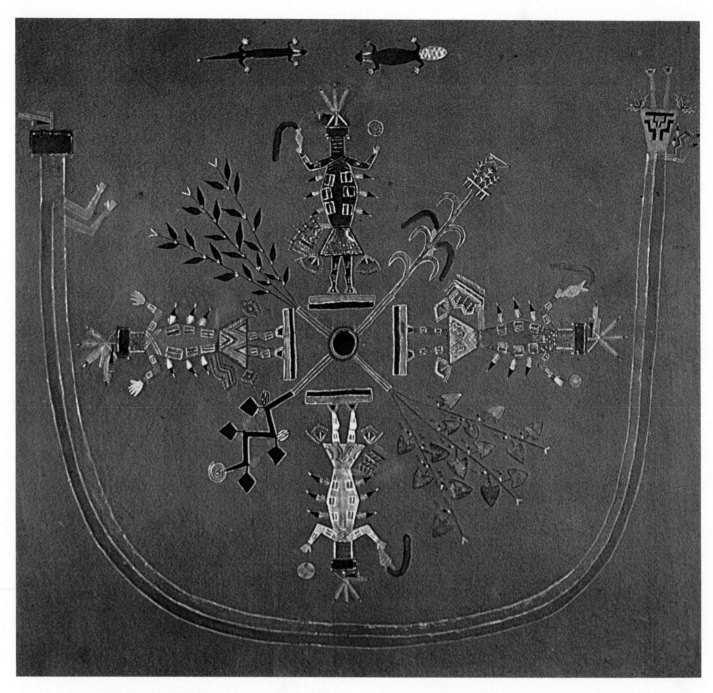

Fish People, Male Shootingway. (No. 8, Walcott catalog; USNM 377474; BAE negative 2457–b–25.)

Sandpaintings of the Navaho Shootingway and The Walcott Collection

Leland C. Wyman

SMITHSONIAN INSTITUTION PRESS

City of Washington

1970

SERIAL PUBLICATIONS OF THE SMITHSONIAN INSTITUTION

The emphasis upon publications as a means of diffusing knowledge was expressed by the first Secretary of the Smithsonian Institution. In his formal plan for the Institution, Joseph Henry articulated a program that included the following statement: "It is proposed to publish a series of reports, giving an account of the new discoveries in science, and of the changes made from year to year in all branches of knowledge not strictly professional." This keynote of basic research has been adhered to over the years in the issuance of thousands of titles in serial publications under the Smithsonian imprint, commencing with *Smithsonian Contributions to Knowledge* in 1848 and continuing with the following active series:

Smithsonian Annals of Flight
Smithsonian Contributions to Anthropology
Smithsonian Contributions to Astrophysics
Smithsonian Contributions to Botany
Smithsonian Contributions to the Earth Sciences
Smithsonian Contributions to Paleobiology
Smithsonian Contributions to Zoology
Smithsonian Studies in History and Technology

In these series, the Institution publishes original articles and monographs dealing with the research and collections of its several museums and offices and of professional colleagues at other institutions of learning. These papers report newly acquired facts, synoptic interpretations of data, or original theory in specialized fields. Each publication is distributed by mailing lists to libraries, laboratories, institutes, and interested specialists throughout the world. Individual copies may be obtained from the Smithsonian Institution Press as long as stocks are available.

S. DILLON RIPLEY
Secretary
Smithsonian Institution

LIBRARY OF CONGRESS CARD 79–603863

U.S. GOVERNMENT PRINTING OFFICE, WASHINGTON : 1970

For sale by the Superintendent of Documents, U.S. Government Printing Office
Washington, D.C. 20402—Price $3.75

ABSTRACT

Wyman, Leland C. Sandpaintings of the Navaho Shootingway and The Walcott Collection. *Smithsonian Contributions to Anthropology*, 13:1–102. 1970.—A brief account of the Navaho and their ceremonial system ("religion") and practice of ritual, with its sanctioning mythology, provides background for the discussion of the sandpaintings of the Shootingway chantway, its Mountain-Shootingway phase, and its Evilway ritual. A short section on the mythology of the male and female branches of Shootingway relates its major mythic motifs to the following account of the symbols and designs of its sandpaintings. Special attention is given to the rarely performed Sun's House phase of male Shootingway and the double sandpainting, Sky-reaching Rock, the most elaborate of all sandpainting designs, which is especially associated with this phase. Finally, there is a detailed descriptive catalog of the 28 reproductions of Navaho sandpaintings in the Mrs. Charles D. Walcott Collection, now in the United States National Museum.

Preface and Acknowledgments

In the pages that follow we will see in a specific situation (the Shootingways) and in a general collection (the Mrs. Charles D. Walcott collection of sandpainting reproductions) how the Navaho priestly practitioner of ritual makes visible in his drypaintings the invisible and thus brings patient, spectators, and himself into the presence of supernatural powers. His apprentices, learning by doing rather than by copying, prepare themselves likewise to be able to harmonize relationships between man and the supernatural through incarnational sacred pictures. Thus the dangerous is brought under control, the sick are cured, and immunity is bestowed.

Drypainting is only one item of the complex symphony of the arts that make up a Navaho song ceremonial. In their chants the Navaho have combined all the major arts which we recognize: music and poetry in the songs and prayers, drama and dance in the ritual acts, graphic art in the drypaintings, great prose and poetry in the myths. The last sanctions and explains all the others, and drypainting, at least in Navaho thinking, illustrates them. All these arts are interrelated in an interlocking system, permeated with colorful symbolism, and always in the last analysis one must have recourse to mythology.

Although to the Navaho a drypainting is a ritual instrument to be used for bringing about certain results, in their own resourceful way they have embellished this art—doubtless borrowed from the somewhat simpler creations of their Pueblo neighbors—until to us it appears to stand at the top among other traditional arts. The innumerable combinations of a limited number of symbols in daring and subtle variations within the frozen limits of ritual prescriptions give evidence of ingenious creativity in the past. Although correctness, lest the instrument be faulty and therefore dangerous, is emphasized by the Navaho informant, there is some evidence, that, mixed with concern for function, there is an esthetic component. The good and the beautiful are inseparable for that which is correctly performed, and therefore useful, cannot be ugly. Moreover, how can we explain the elaboration of sandpaintings beyond a merely functional level—with concern for the artistic devices of balance between darks and lights, symmetry, contrast, and other similar aspects—on other than esthetic grounds? Sandpaintings are truely concrete embodiments of that untranslatable term which describes everything that the Navaho thinks is good and favorable to man, and which we render "beautiful" for want of a more inclusive word in English. Perhaps "harmony" would be a better rendering, for the words derived from this Navaho stem cover such things as harmony, perfection, goodness, normality, success, blessedness, order, peace, prosperity, happiness—in short everything that man desires. It is the Navaho's basic value concept, the center of their religious thought.

The strewing of loose dry pigments to make impermanent pictures, although not a common art, is a world-wide practice. Numerous other Indian tribes used drypaintings: the Navaho's linguistic relatives the Apache, various Pueblo groups, a number of California tribes, and some Plains Indians. In India and Tibet ground painting, both sacred and secular, is practised. The art has even appeared in Christianity, for drypaintings are made

on the floors of churches in some parts of Mexico during religious fiestas. Nowhere, however, is there wealth of content, variety of artistic devices, or excellence of technique, equal
to that of the Navaho. The Pueblo Indians of the Southwest make rather simple drypaintings on the altars in their ceremonial chambers, the kivas, and there are resemblances
between Navaho sandpaintings, and certain elements of prehistoric mural paintings on
the walls of ancient Pueblo kivas uncovered by archeologists. It is presumed, therefore, that
the Athabaskan ancestors of the Navaho borrowed this art and elaborated its content and
artistry as they did other borrowed traits, such as weaving. Unfortunately we have no
materials for studying the evolution of the art in Navaho hands, for the first sandpaintings
ever recorded and preserved, in 1887, were as fully developed as those used today.

One consequence of conversation during a social visit in 1963 with my friend the late
Frank H. H. Roberts, Jr., then director of the Bureau of American Ethnology, was the
suggestion that I write a descriptive catalog of the Mrs. Charles D. Walcott collection of
reproductions of Navaho Indian sandpaintings in the United States National Museum.
After Frank's death in 1966, Richard B. Woodbury, then chairman of the Office of Anthropology, Smithsonian Institution, encouraged me to go ahead with the project, and I am
most indebted to him and to Saul H. Riesenberg, present chairman of the Office of Anthropology, and to Mrs. Margaret C. Blaker, archivist of the National Anthropological Archives,
Smithsonian Institution, for providing me with photographs, copies of correspondence and
notes, and other materials pertaining to the collection.

My warmest thanks go to Edward B. Danson, director of the Museum of Northern
Arizona, and to various members of the staff of the research center of that museum (where
most of this work was written) for providing necessary facilities. I am also mindful of the
courteous assistance given me at the Museum of Navaho Ceremonial Art in Santa Fe by the
late Kenneth E. Foster, who was director of the museum, and by his successor, Bertha P.
Dutton, during the numerous periods when I worked with the collections there. Also, I
appreciate certain physical facilities provided to me as professor emeritus by Boston
University.

David P. McAllester of Wesleyan University generously gave me copies of his field
notes concerning the Sun's House phase of Shootingway and also assisted in the prepara-
tion of the section of the manuscript concerned with that aspect of the chant. David M.
Brugge, anthropologist for the Navajo Land Claim at Window Rock, Arizona, provided
information concerning Matthew M. Murphy, the collector of the paintings now in the
Mrs. Charles D. Walcott Collection. An appeal to Mrs. Lita Osmundsen, director of
research, Wenner-Gren Foundation for Anthropological Research, resulted in financial
assistance for the typing of the manuscript, a task which Mrs. Barabara Miranda of Bel-
mont, Massachusetts, performed with her usual assiduous care. Frederick W. Maynard of
the department of biology, Boston University, assisted in preparing the illustrations. My
own labors were lightened by my wife, Paula, who helped with the reading of the
manuscript.

I am indebted to the following individuals and institutions for permission to illustrate
reproductions of sandpaintings under their care or in their collections: Bertha P. Dutton,
director, Museum of Navaho Ceremonial Art (plates 13, 14, 37–42, 44); Museum of
Northern Arizona (Plates 10, 15, 16); Anna-Britta Hellbom, curator, Etnografiska Museet,
Stockholm (Plate 12); Professor Horace L. Friess, Bush Collection of Religion and Culture,
Columbia University (Plate 36); and George H. Ewing, curator in charge, division of
research, Museum of New Mexico (Plate 43).

I have used abbreviations of names of museums and shortened forms of the names of
the various collections as follows:

ASM: Arizona State Museum, Tucson, Arizona.
Bush: Bush Collection of Religion and Culture, at Columbia University, New York City.
Dendahl: Henry Dendahl Collection, Coronado Building, Santa Fe, New Mexico.
Ganado: Paintings by Red Point (Miguelito) collected by the late Ramon Hubbell and now in the
                Hubbell Trading Post National Historic Site or in the possession of Mrs. Ramon Hubbell,
                Scottsdale, Arizona.

Haile:	Father Berard Haile Collection, in Museum of Northern Arizona, Flagstaff.
Harvey:	Katherine M. Harvey Collection, in Museum of Northern Arizona.
Huckel:	John Frederick Huckel Collection, in Taylor Museum, Colorado Springs, Colorado.
MNA:	Museum of Northern Arizona.
MNCA:	Museum of Navaho Ceremonial Art, Santa Fe, New Mexico.
MNM:	Museum of New Mexico, Santa Fe.
Newcomb:	Collection of Franc Johnson Newcomb, Albuquerque, New Mexico.
Oakes:	Maud Oakes Collection, now mostly in Museum of Navaho Ceremonial Art.
Reichard:	Gladys A. Reichard Collection, in Museum of Northern Arizona.
Stockholm:	Paintings by Red Point (Miguelito) in Etnografiska Museet, Stockholm, Sweden.
USNM:	United States National Museum, Washington, D.C.
Walcott:	Mrs. Charles D. Walcott Collection, in United States National Museum.
Wetherill:	Wetherill Collection, in Museum of Northern Arizona.
Woodard:	Collection of M. L. Woodard, Gallup, New Mexico.

LELAND C. WYMAN
Boston University
Boston, Massachusetts

Contents

Tables

Illustrations

(PLATES 1–44 follow Page 50)

Sandpaintings of the Navaho Shootingway
and The Walcott Collection

The Navaho and Their Religion

The Navaho Indian tribe, the largest group of native Americans in the United States, numbering more than 110,000 individuals, continues to be one of the most rapidly growing ethnic groups in this country. Its members have overflowed the legal boundaries of their approximately 18 million acres of reservation and leased lands, some having been resettled on other reservations and others having relocated in some of our industrial centers. Their homeland—the severely eroded Colorado plateau country of the "four corners" region of northeastern Arizona, northwestern New Mexico, southwestern Colorado, and southeastern Utah—although containing some of the most beautiful scenic attractions in the world, is singularly inhospitable for those who have to make a living from it. Attempts to cope with this situation have resulted in a relatively enormous number of acculturative changes in the last few decades, so that on their lands Navaho Indians now operate motels, restaurants, service stations, an industrial park (near Gallup, New Mexico), an $8 million lumber mill, extensive irrigation projects, and tribal parks patterned after our national parks and monuments. Moreover, they have attracted to their lands a number of small industries that employ Navaho labor. Among other projects is the establishment of a Navaho Community College on the reservation.

In spite of these changes and in spite of their having overcome to a large extent their distrust of the white man's medicine (most Navaho babies are now born in hospitals or in clinics), the Navaho have preserved the traditional cultural inventory of their body of beliefs and practices dealing with those segments of experience not subject to rational control—or what

NOTE. The spelling "Navaho" is used herein because this paper was in press at the time the American Anthropological Association announced that it will use "Navajo" in its publications. Such usage is in line with a recent resolution of the Advisory Committee of the Navaho Tribal Council. In future publications the Smithsonian Institution Press will use the recommended spelling, "Navajo." [Editor.]

we would call their "philosophy" and their "religion." This cultural complex encompasses as well their system of medical theory and practice—a system which provides comfort, social security, potent psychotherapy, and some actual medical therapy to a people predisposed to worry over health. There is no doubt that it was this predisposition—exacerbated by the prevalence of disease, hard times, and the fear of ghosts and witchcraft—that caused the Navaho's religious practice to take the form of curing ceremonials. In nearly every one of their religious performances an actual patient is treated for a real or anticipated ailment. Their priests are also their doctors There is no word in the Navaho language that can be translated as "religion," but this word from our own culture is the most convenient label for their beliefs concerning the dynamics of the universe and techniques for controlling them and their belief in what we would call "the supernatural," although they do not make it a separate category of thought as we do. Traditional Navaho ceremonialism may be undergoing, however, what will prove to be a losing battle with the peyote cult, the Native American Church of North America, a redemptive social movement which rejects local traditional culture and which in turn is rejected by cultural conservatives. In the 1950s the proportion of Navaho peyotists varied from zero to 80 percent of the population in different areas of the reservation, and today the proportion probably is much higher. The recent book by David F. Aberle (1966) provides the most extensive study of this question.

The core of Navaho religious philosophy is the belief that the universe is an orderly, all-inclusive, unity of interrelated elements in which the principle of reciprocity governs man's relations with these elements, which include other men. Thus, favor for favor and injury for injury, unless compensated for, are the keynotes that should guide man's behavior. Being all-inclusive, the universe contains both good and evil, not as abstract ethical concepts but as complementary

1

components. Innumerable powers in it are indifferent or good when under control and in harmony with man, but they may be potentially evil when uncontrolled. Some, such as ghosts of the dead or certain beings or elements like snake, lightning, or coyote, have greater potentiality for evil than others; and some are predominently good unless related to excessive activity. Improper contact with inherently dangerous powers—even though it be indirect, unintentional, or unconscious—or the breaching of traditional restrictions (taboos) may lead to illness, the price man pays for disturbance of the normal order, harmony, or balance among elements in the universe. Such a theory of evil is based on contagion rather than sin; for example, murder is potentially dangerous not because of the deed itself but because of contact with the dead. Likewise, excesses in gambling or in sexual activity—in fact, any excessive activity—are thought of as symptoms of disease amenable to ritual cure, and thus are not considered sins. Malevolent misuse of ritual knowledge by witches causes troubles that are especially difficult to deal with, sometimes being refractory to ceremonial treatment and requiring special techniques such as the sucking cure (see Haile, 1950). The witch, therefore, is hated and feared.

The Ceremonial System

The means for bringing dangerous elements under control, exorcising ghosts, restoring harmony, curing disease, and rendering the patient immune to further contamination from the same supernatural influences are the knowledge and correct performance of orderly procedures; that is, control by ritual. In a ceremonial, the Holy People, the supernatural beings invoked, are the judges of the completeness and correctness of the ritual, and if satisfied they are compelled by the ethic of reciprocity to restore universal harmony and thus cure the patient. Hence, prayers and offerings in Navaho ceremonials are invocatory and compulsive, to attract and obligate the holy ones, not to glorify or thank them.

Navaho ceremonials are conducted by trained specialists, called "singers," because the singing which accompanies every important act in the ritual is held to be the one essential element of the ceremonial. The singers learn by apprenticeship, ratifying their knowledge by payment to the teacher. A singer specializes in one or two (or at most half a dozen) complete chants, because each one is a vast complex of songs, prayers, ritual acts, plant medicines, material properties, and symbols. The chants have two-night, five-night, and some even nine-night forms. The singer is paid according to the elaborateness of the

ceremonial, and by reciprocity he is compelled to perform if he accepts the fee. Conversely, it is the payment which insures the efficacy of the performance. The cost of a ceremonial may vary from the equivalent of 25 dollars for a two-night performance to several thousand dollars for a nine-night chant when hundreds of spectators must be hospitably fed by the sponsors—the patient and his kinsmen. Navaho singers do not belong to organized priesthoods, and they have no religious societies like their neighbors, the Pueblo Indians, and no religious calendar, but they carry out the ceremonials whenever they are needed. In fact, there is no sense of membership in anything like a church. One merely uses the ceremonials or one does not.

A singer is summoned by an intermediary, usually a kinsman of the patient, after the family has held a conference and decided upon the etiological factors causing the patient's illness—bad dreams, fear of the consequences of violated taboos, or other indication that he requires ritual aid. If it cannot determine which ceremonial is needed, the family may employ a diagnostician, a specialist in divination (usually not a singer) who interprets involuntary motions made by his hand while he is in a trance-like state (hand-trembling). Sometimes, but not commonly, the older techniques of star-gazing or listening, interpreting things seen or heard, are used. Unless there is urgency, the singer usually comes to the family's home (which has been emptied and swept for the chant) within four days. Only the traditional, roughly circular house (hogan) may be used. Square houses such as our own, which are becoming more and more common, will not suffice for the ceremony. The Navahos have never built towns like those of the Pueblos, but live in little family groups, often scattered far apart over the semidesert terrain.

The Navaho ceremonial system consists of two types of ceremonials, the chantways, performances in which the songs are accompanied by a rattle, and those in which a rattle is not used which we call rites for lack of a single Navaho equivalent term for them. Among the latter are two song ceremonial complexes of great importance, the Blessingway rites and the Enemyway rite. Blessingway, regarded by the Navaho as the backbone of their religion and given historical precedence over all other ceremonials by them, controls all the chantways and provides a unifying force in Navaho culture. Comparatively short and simple, lasting only two nights, the Blessingway rites consist of songs, prayers, a ceremonial bath, and, sometimes, drypaintings. They are performed to maintain harmony, to avert misfortune, for good luck, to invoke blessings upon all of man's possessions and activities. A person who is sung over represents the group to be benefited. The Blessingway rites are used for the installation of tribal officers, for the departing or returning soldier, for the neophyte who is singing for the first time, for blessing a new house, for consecrating ceremonial paraphernalia, and to aid childbirth. The girl's adolescence rite and the wedding ceremony are Blessingway rites, and so was the obsolete rain ceremony. Every chant includes at least one Blessingway song to adjust possible mistakes and errors which might otherwise render the ceremonial ineffectual or even cause illness.

The Enemyway rite (sometimes included with the Evilway chants) is used to exorcise the ghosts of aliens (non-Navahos), and it makes much of war and violence. In fact, it belongs in the native category of ceremonials which may be translated Evilway, and in Navaho theory it should have nothing to do with Blessingway, which emphasizes peace and harmony, excluding all evil. Such rites are discussed in detail and three versions of the myth of Blessingway are presented in a publication by Wyman (1970). It is possible that the understandably obsolescent hunting (Gameway), salt-gathering, and war rites drew upon Blessingway and Enemyway for their songs.

The Navaho think of certain ceremonials as "going together" or as "partner chants." They make such associations because of interrelations in the origin legends of the chants, efficacy against common etiological factors, procedures peculiar to the group, and so on. Although all Navahos in all regions do not group these ceremonials in precisely the same way, the uniformity among the groupings and subgroupings of chants is striking enough to enable us to derive a classification from the remarks of informants (see Wyman and Kluckhohn, 1938).

Each of the chants used to cure illness is concerned with particular etiological factors that are thought to cause the disease or diseases for which the chant is believed to be efficacious. For instance, Mountainway—a chant in the Holyway group (see below)—deals with mountain creatures (such as bear, porcupine, and weasel) as etiological factors; thus, it is used for mental disturbances ("bear sickness") and genitourinary and gastrointestinal ailments ("porcupine sickness"). The relationships of all the various chants to particular etiological factors and diseases have been described in numerous publications; moreover, some information on such matters is presented later on in this paper in connection with the discussion of items in the Walcott collection of sandpainting reproductions—for example, numbers 23 (Big Starway), 24 (Beautyway), 26 (Nightway), 27 (Plumeway), and 28 (Navaho Windway).

Most of the chantways are dominated by a ritual or pattern of behavior governing procedure that is concerned with restoration and the attraction of good, a ritual which may be translated as Holyway. A few of them may also be performed according to Evilway (or Ghostway) ritual, characterized by acts designed to exorcise native ghosts and thus cure sickness caused by them, and, hopefully, to combat the effects of witchcraft. Such activities include big hoop and cincture or garment ceremonies, overshooting, blackening the patient, and lightning-herb, ash-blowing, and brushing procedures (see Wyman, 1965, pp. 31–42, 58–62). A few may also be conducted according to Lifeway ritual, specialized for curing injuries resulting from accidents. A distinctive feature of Lifeway ritual is painting the patient red, the color of flesh and blood, symbolizing return to life and health. In addition there is a fundamental Evilway chant called Upward-reachingway and a fundamental Lifeway chant called Flintway (see Wyman and Kluckhohn, 1938). Formerly there were about 23 Holyway chantway systems, all for curing illnesses, to which—by elaboration according to male and female branches, ritual, and other considerations—about 40 names for song ceremonials could be ascribed. Ten or eleven of these chantways are now extinct or obsolescent, and four or five are uncommon, leaving only eight that are well known and frequently performed.

Each chantway has special relations with certain groups of supernatural beings, although there is considerable overlapping. The organization of the Navaho pantheon presents perplexing problems. There is no evidence of a well-ordered hierarchy, although Reichard (1950) suggested that a sun cult is outstanding. Factors that complicate the picture are the equivalence of beings appearing under different names or as various actors in the myths, the multiplication of deities in time and space, duplication of functions among different deities, and, perhaps most important, the immanence of supernatural power. Animals, plants, mountains, and many natural phenomena are endowed with power. Even the seemingly most insignificant of these are indispensable; all are interdependent, being complementary parts of the whole. Animals and plants are conceived as capable of assuming human form at will, mountains have anthropomorphic inner forms, and even material objects such as arrows may be "people" (see Wyman, 1970).

Among the Holy People (powerful and dangerous, not virtuously holy), Changing Woman is surely the most beloved. Her twin children Monster Slayer and Born for Water, sired by the Sun, represent war power. First Man, First Woman, First Boy, and First Girl and their companions Coyote, the exponent of irresponsibility, and Be'gochidi were prominent in early events on the earth just after the Emergence from the underworlds. Members of a group of Holy People led by Talking God and known as the Ye'i are impersonated by masked dancers in public performances of some ceremonials. The list of Holy People representing the powers in the world—Bear, Big Snake, Cactus People, Ant People, Thunders, Winds, and a host of others—is endless. Nearly every element in the universe may be thus personalized, and even the least of these personalizations, such as Big Fly and Cornbeetle Girl (tiny helpers and mentors), are as necessary for the harmonious scheme of things as is the great Sun.

The Navaho ceremonial system is sanctioned and explained in a large body of oral "literature" transmitted from generation to generation around family firesides (see Spencer, 1957; Wyman, 1962, pp. 29–58). This mythology consists of two major parts—the general Origin Myth, which includes the story of the Emergence from the underworlds (see Wyman, 1965, pp. 74–93), and the Origin Legends of the separate ceremonials that branch off from the Origin Myth at various points. These legends tell how the chant started and how it should be carried out. There are as many of these ceremonial myths as there are ceremonials and branches thereof, but they are not entirely independent. Besides the unique mythic motifs specific to given ceremonials, there are rather complex episodes (major motifs) that appear in the myths of two or more ceremonials, a host of simple incidents (minor motifs) that are common to many chantways, and some universal elements that are present in all or virtually all myths. Thus the Navaho's mythology, like their pantheon and, indeed, their universe, is a unit composed of interlocking parts, filled with vivid word imagery, fine ritual poetry, keen humor, and great imaginative power. The myth of Blessingway is one that is most intimately associated with the Origin Myth, being mostly concerned with the Post-Emergence Events and giving the origin of many elements of Navaho culture (see Wyman, 1970). It is felt that a singer should know the myths pertaining to his specialty ceremonials, and that when relating one he should begin with the Origin Myth and tell it up to where the chant myth branches from it. Such knowledge is not, however, an indispensable part of a singer's equipment, although the best singers do learn the myths.

The Holyway Chants

Holyway chants may be categorized in seven subgroups: the Shooting Chant, Mountain Chant, God-Impersonators, Wind Chant, Hand-Tremblingway, and Eagle Trapping subgroups, and a grouping of three extinct ceremonials of uncertain affiliation. The Mountain Chant subgroup, one of the largest, contains the Mountainways, Beautyway, and the obsolescent or extinct Excessway and the related Mothway. The God-Impersonators subgroup includes the well-known Nightways, the related Big Godway, Plumeway, the obsolescent Coyoteway, and the extinct Dogway and Ravenway. The Wind Chant subgroup is made up of Navaho Windway and Chiricahua Windway. Hand-Tremblingway stands alone. The Eagle Trapping subgroup contains the uncommon or obsolescent Eagleway and Beadway.

The Shooting Chant subgroup contains the Shootingways, which are treated in detail below, the less commonly performed Red Antway, Big Starway (performed today according to Evilway ritual), and the recently extinct Hailway and Waterway.

Red Antway is concerned with diseases coming from ants, horned toads, and, secondarily, from lightning and bears; such diseases are primarily of a genitourinary nature, although other conditions—such as gastrointestinal distress, skin diseases, sore throat, or rheumatism—may be treated by the chant (see Wyman, 1965, pp. 25–27). Big Starway, although probably concerned with heavenly bodies originally, being an Evilway chant, today is used to treat almost any illness supposed to be caused by the Ghosts of Navahos or by witches (see Wheelwright, 1956, pp. 106–110). The extinct Hailway and Waterway were used to treat injuries caused by frost or water.

The Windways may belong in the Shooting Chant subgroup instead of comprising a separate one, as there are numerous conformities among the major mythic motifs of the origin legends of the two subgroups (see Wyman, 1962, p. 46, table 2, pp. 48, 66). Moreover, among the etiological factors against which Navaho Windway is directed are snakes and sometimes lightning (Thunder), with which snakes (and arrows) are conceptually equated, and such factors are the main concern of Shootingway (see Wyman, 1962, pp. 20–21). Another ceremonial which seems to be closely related to Shootingway, again on the basis of the origin myths, is Flintway, the fundamental Lifeway chant, which Kluckhohn (1960, p. 69) did assign to the Shooting Chant subgroup (see also Wyman, 1962, p. 51). It may be significant that Shootingway frequently is performed according to Lifeway ritual.

A curing chant is made up of procedures that invoke and attract supernatural beings who can correct the harm done by them or by their earthly cognates, and other procedures that exorcise evil. Some of these ceremonies are more or less fixed while others may be inserted or omitted, or modified according to circumstances. Moreover, any of them may be modified internally according to the specific symbolism of the chant being given.

A typical Holyway chant consists of about twelve such ceremonies. It begins at sundown when the singer consecrates the hogan by placing cornmeal and sprigs of hard oak on or above the roof beams in the cardinal directions. Following this, and on each of the three succeeding evenings in a four-night or nine-night chant, there may be an unraveling ceremony, in which a certain number of bundles of herbs and feathers tied together with a wool string are applied to various parts of the patient's body and the string is pulled free, symbolizing release from harm. Then there is a short singing ceremony, sometimes accompanied by basket drumming (beating an inverted basket), that goes on for an hour or so.

The most spectacular feature of a Holyway chant is the sandpainting ceremony. It is performed once in a two-night ceremonial and four times—on successive days, and each time with a painting of a different design—in a five-night or nine-night chant. If the chant is to include this feature, a setting-out ceremony is performed just before dawn on the first morning. Bundle-prayersticks (wooden sticks decorated with painted symbols and feathers) are vertically inserted in a mound of earth in front of the door to the hogan to notify human and supernatural beings that a sandpainting is to be made. A fire is kindled with a firedrill, and coals from it are used to rekindle the fire throughout the chant. Then, just after dawn on each of the first four mornings a sweat and emetic ceremony drives away evil by internal and external purification. During that ceremony small sandpaintings, often of snakes, may be made at the cardinal points around the central fireplace, and another small sandpainting made northwest of the fire, on which the patient's basket of emetic is placed. Ritually prepared wooden pokers are laid beside the sandpaintings around the fire. Sweating, vomiting, and bathing in the warm herbal decoction (emetic) purify the patient and others who may wish to participate. After breakfast, invocatory offerings of "jewels" (bits of turquoise, etc.), painted reeds stuffed with tobacco ("cigarettes"), and/or painted wooden prayersticks are prepared to attract the Holy People. The patient holds these while repeating a long litany after the singer. Finally, a helper deposits the offerings in specified places away from the hogan.

In the forenoon of the last day a bath ceremony purifies the patient still further. Following this, or after the offering ceremonies on the other days, the sandpainting within the hogan is begun. When the picture has been completed, usually in the late forenoon or early afternoon, the bundle-prayersticks are brought in from the set-out mound and placed in upright position around the painting. Cornmeal then is sprinkled on the sandpainting by singer and patient.

On the last day only, the patient's body is painted from head to foot with symbolic designs by means of mineral pigments (figure painting), and in his hair are tied a feather plume and a shell or turquoise bead (token tying). The bead becomes the patient's property, a mark of recognition for the Holy People and a protection from further danger. The patient then sits on some figure in the sandpainting; and the singer, after moistening his palms in herb medicine, applies sand from various parts of the painted figures's bodies to corresponding parts of the patient's body. Then he similarly applies the bundle-prayersticks and parts of his own body to the patient. Finally, the patient leaves the hogan; the sandpainting is erased; and the sand is carried outside and deposited to the north of the hogan.

The procedures in the ritual identify the patient with the Holy People represented in the painting who have been attracted to the scene to look at their painted likenesses. The patient absorbs their powers from the sands applied to him, exchanging evil for good, and becomes strong like them and immune to further harm. Indeed, for a time he is a Holy Person himself. That is why he must observe four days of ceremonial restrictions afterwards, lest he harm others through his acquired power.

There is an all-night singing on the final night, and at dawn the patient faces the east outside the hogan and "breathes in the dawn" four times. The ceremonial ends with a final prayer and a Blessingway song to avert the consequences of errors of omission or commission.

Optional ceremonies such as the ritual consumption of cornmeal mush or a meat decoction, or the performance of a shock rite (see Wyman, 1965, pp. 56–58), may be added at extra expense if requested by the patient. Public performances by teams of masked dancers impersonating the Holy People or other exhibitions—like a sacred vaudeville show (Dark Circle of Branches, "Corral Dance" or "Fire Dance")–may occupy the final night of nine-night performances of some chants, such as Nightway and Mountainway.

Nearly every act throughout a ceremonial is accompanied by singing. The singer leads, shaking a rattle, while all who can join in. Most chants require knowledge of several hundred songs. Prayers are said at intervals; herbal medicines are prepared and administered to the patient; a bullroarer is whirled to imitate thunder; the singer's equipment is laid out on a calico spread and objects from it are applied to the patient; and expendable materials and objects are deposited somewhere outside the hogan where they can do no harm. Some ceremonies, such as the consecration of the hogan, the bath, figure painting, token tying, all-night singing, and the dawn procedures occur only once in any chant. Others are repeated four times in five-night or nine-night performances but are given only once in a two-night chant—except for the sweat-emetic ceremony, which must be performed four times if at all. In a nine-night chant the short singing, setting-out, and sandpainting ceremonies are moved ahead, to the fifth to eighth days.

Sandpaintings

The sandpaintings are made by trickling dry pigments from between the thumb and flexed forefinger onto a background of clean, tan-colored sand which has been smoothed with a weaving batten. The pigments are red, yellow, and white sandstone, and charcoal that has been finely pulverized on a grinding stone, and a few mixtures—such as charcoal and white sand for blue, charcoal and red sand for brown, and red and white sand for pink.[1] Drypainting is a more accurate name for the process because charcoal is not sand, and Blessingway paintings are made entirely of dry pigments of vegetable origin. Any male person who knows how may help (under the direction of the singer who seldom takes part himself except to lay out some preliminary lines) in the making of a drypainting. Women do not participate for fear of injury from the supernatural powers invoked.

The resulting picture may vary in size from one that is a foot or less in diameter to one that occupies most of the floor of the hogan, or sometimes to one more than 20 feet across that required the building of a special hogan to accommodate it. The average sandpainting, about six feet in diameter, is made by from four to six men who have worked from three to five hours. When the Holy People taught the human heroes of the myths how to make drypaintings they forbade their reproduction in permanent form lest they be soiled or damaged, so the painters have only their memories to guide them. Consequently, most of the reproductions in collections in our museums have been made by white people. Only a few Navahos have dared to defy the supernatural injunctions, and the creator of the paintings in the Walcott collection was one of these.

The main theme symbols of drypaintings represent the human protagonist of the myth and the Holy People he encounters in his adventures and who are concerned with his instruction. The symbols may represent supernatural beings always depicted in human form, but more often they represent anthropomorphized powers abounding in the world—animals, plants, natural phenomena, geographic features such as mountains, or even material objects. Hence, we are made to see snake, bear, ant, cactus, corn, wind, hail, or arrow "people," and many others. These powers may also be represented in more or less naturalistic forms, and there are accepted symbols for natural phenomena, heavenly bodies, mythological creatures, and the like.

Sandpaintings might be thought of as illustrations of Navaho mythology, but few of them are actually narrative in our terms; rather, they indicate action mainly by symbols. Anyone familiar with the symbolism and the myths, however, can read them and thus be reminded of episodes in the sacred tales (see Wyman, 1959, pp. 11–12). The main theme symbols, with a few exceptions, are arranged according to one of three types of composition: *linear*, with figures in a row or rows, repeated to increase power, often standing on a locality bar (usually black, representing the earth); *radial*, with important symbols cardinally oriented in the form of a Greek cross and with subsidiary symbols in the quadrants in the form of a Saint Andrew's cross, around a "center" symbolizing a locality (a spring, pool, mountain, or dwelling) where the commemorated episode took place; and *extended center*, with a central motif occupying most of the space (see Wyman, 1960, p. 24; 1962, pp. 277–278; 1965, p. 208).

Symbols often occur in pairs or multiples of pairs called male and female, representing differences in power. Sequences of colors have sexual or directional significance. The symbols are combined in various ways in different paintings both for ritual and for artistic reasons, but always in a prescribed manner, for they are powerful and dangerous if mishandled. An encircling *guardian* (usually the Rainbow supernatural) is made to surround the whole picture, with an opening to the east for the exchange of good and evil with the world outside. Sometimes control of this eastern aperture is enhanced by the painting of small *paired guardians*, often Big Fly or Ripener Girl, in it.

There is no way of determining how many designs are known and used today, but more than 500 different designs have been recorded by collectors. Moreover, the results of a count would depend upon the point of view, ours or that of the Navaho. Designs that we might call very different may appear to be the same to the Navaho eye. For instance, to us a radial

---

[1] The technique, materials, nature, and use of Navaho sandpaintings have been described so many times since 1887—when Washington Matthews published the first colored reproductions—that only a few references to such descriptions will suffice here: Matthews (1887, 1902); Newcomb and Reichard (1937, pp. 18–24); Reichard (1939, pp. 14–25); Kluckhohn and Wyman (1940, pp. 45, 61–62, 69, 83, 93–100); Wyman (1952; 1959; 1960, pp. 13–25; 1962, pp. 275–278; 1965, pp. 206–208; 1970, p. 65); Foster (1964).

composition looks entirely different from a linear one, but if both portray Snake People or buffalo a Navaho might regard them as identical. On the other hand, a slight change, such as making a snake's tongue red instead of yellow, might be unnoticeable to us but would constitute an important difference for a Navaho (see Wyman, 1962, pp. 278, 280–284; 1965, p. 207).

All Holyway chants are known (or are alleged) to have used sandpaintings; most or perhaps all of the Evilway chants have or had them; and Blessingway rites employ drypaintings made of corn meal, corn and other plant pollens, powdered flower petals, and charcoal strewn on a plain sand background or on a buckskin or a cloth substitute. For some chants, scarcely more designs are known today than the four needed for a five-night or nine-night performance, while for others, such as Shootingway, there may be about 100. For a given ceremonial, the singer selects one or four of those he knows, according to his or the the patient's wishes, the etiological factors supposed to have caused the disease being treated, or some such consideration.

In summary, the purpose of the drypainted pictures of Holy People and their activities is, first, to attract these beings (for they enjoy seeing their portraits made) so that they may help to cure the patient. Secondly, the sacred pictures are used to identifiy the patient with the Holy People by seating him on the figures and applying their sands to his body. Finally, this procedure provides a two-way path (between the patient and the symbols in sand) for the exchange of good and evil, health and sickness, immunity and susceptibility; thus; man is enabled to partake of the nature of divinity.

Shootingway

The Shootingways were said by Miguelito (also known as Red Point), a famous specialist in such chants, to be the root and key of Navaho religion. Of course this statement was influenced by the feeling of a singer for his specialty, but it is true that the Shootingways are among the most popular and most frequently performed song ceremonials today. Moreover, they have preserved more of the elements of a chantway complex and have more sandpaintings associated with them than has any other ceremonial. All of this argues for their fundamental character.

The Shootingway chantway complex has more ramifications in regard to rituals, subrituals, phases, branches, and etiological factors than any other chantway (See Wyman and Kluckhohn, 1938, pp. 5, 11, 21, 23; Haile, 1947b, pp. 9–10; Wyman, 1952 p. 34; 1960, p. 37). It is mainly concerned with the alleviation of diseases or other troubles attributed to the effects of thunder and lightning or their cognate symbols, snakes and arrows. Chest and lung troubles and gastrointestinal diseases frequently may be ascribed to these factors, but almost any ailment may be traced to them at the dictation of convenience. Performed according to Evilway ritual, Shootingway deals with conditions attributed to influences from native ghosts, such as insomnia, anorexia, bad dreams, loss of weight, or similar alarming symptoms or feelings (Haile, 1950, pp. viii–x).

MYTHOLOGY

Since sandpaintings could be regarded as illustrations for the stories of Navaho mythology it is appropriate to include a short section on the myths of Shootingway in this work on the paintings (see Wyman, 1960, p. 24). The relationship between the myths and the paintings has been brought out very thoroughly in two elaborate books on the sandpaintings of Shootingway (Newcomb and Reichard, 1937, and Reichard, 1939), so little need be added on that subject; however, since an organized account of the motifs of the myths has not been published heretofore, descriptions and tabulations of such motifs are presented below.

The myths of the Shootingways are excellent examples of the standard pattern of plot construction of Navaho chantway myths (Spencer, 1957, p. 21; Wyman, 1962, p. 29). A hero who gets into a series of predicaments acquires ceremonial knowledge, power, and paraphernalia while various supernatural beings restore, rescue, or protect him. Then he usually makes numerous visits to different Holy People to obtain additional knowledge, power, and paraphernalia. Having accumulated enough such assets to establish a chantway with which he can protect himself, he returns to his people, teaches the ceremonial, and finally departs to live with the supernaturals—or, having become ill from his misadventures, he himself is treated by means of the ceremonial.

The heroes of the Shootingway myths are the Slayer Twins (Monster Slayer and his brother Born-for-Water) or their counterparts, Holy Man and Holy Boy. Sometimes the Slayer Twins are the heroes in the first part of the myth and Holy Man and Holy Boy take over later. The older brother, Monster Slayer or Holy Young Man, is often the real hero, while the younger brother plays a supporting role. In any case, Born-for-Water is never separated from Monster Slayer, and the two are thought of as one (Haile, 1947a, p. 62). When multiplied into a quartet the counterpart of the older brother is usually called

Reared-in-the-Earth (Reared Underground, Reared-in-the-Mountain) while that of the younger brother is called Changing Grandchild. Some singers, however, reverse these identifications. Reichard (1950, p. 55) thought that when the twins are arrayed in armor (in sandpaintings) they are the Slayer Twins but when unarmored they represent Holy Man and Holy Boy.

Fragments of Shootingway myths are scattered here and there in the literature, but we have comparatively few complete versions. Fortunately, however, extensive native texts (by Blue Eyes and Gray Man, see below) for both rituals of Male Shootingway (Holyway and Evilway) have been recorded and translated by expert linguists. There are three versions of the myth of Male Shootingway Holyway and two of Evilway. In the following listing of the five versions the English rendering of the nickname of the Navaho author is followed by his home locality. Red Point, Woman Singer's Son, Gray Man, and Jim Smith derived their information either directly or indirectly from Blue Eyes, who was the great authority on Shootingway in his time.

Blue (Gray) Eyes, Lukachukai Arizona. Holyway ritual. (Recorded by Father Berard Haile, O.F.M., 1924; translated by Gladys A. Reichard, 1928; shorter form published in Newcomb and Reichard, 1937, pp. 25–41 and, excerpts published in Reichard, 1934, pp. 169–179, 194–197.)

Red Point (Miguelito), White Sands, six miles south of Ganado, Arizona. Holyway and Evilway rituals, combined. (Recorded in English by Herman Schweizer, 1924; interpreted by Sam Day, Jr.; shorter form published in Reichard, 1939, pp. 38–73.)

Woman Singer's Son, Red Rock Valley, Arizona. Holyway ritual. (Recorded In English by Mary C. Wheelwright, 1932; shorter, modified form, published in Wheelwright, 1958, pp. 15–23.)

Gray Man, Many Young Cottonwoods Place, Chinle Wash, near Fraser's old store, Arizona. Evilway ritual. (Recorded and translated by Father Berard Haile, 1933; interpreted by Albert G. Sandoval, Lukachukai, Arizona; text and translation published in Haile, 1950.)

Jim Smith (Policeman), Beautiful Valley (or Ganado), Arizona. Evilway ritual. (Recorded and translated by Gladys A. Reichard, 1936; interpreted by Adolph Bitanny.)

The distribution of the major mythic motifs within the five versions of the myth of Male Shootingway is shown in Table 1.

Only one myth of Female Shootingway Holyway is on record. It is a brief story (about 1,900 words) by Woman Singer of Two Grey Hills, New Mexico, that was told to Mary C. Wheelwright in 1932 (see Wyman, 1962, p. 66). The recorder noted that Woman Singer, who was the sister of Blue Eyes, stated that her knowledge came from "her home, near Chee Dodge's house, near Crystal," New Mexico. The myth is recorded in English. Another brief story (about 2,200 words) that was recorded in English by Louisa Wade Wetherill (1906–1909) has virtually the same content as that of

Woman Singer, so it too is probably a myth of Female Shootingway although it is labeled merely "the Shooting Chant." Mrs. Wetherill's note on this story reads "told me by H. H.," who could have been Hastin Hoskinini of Oljeto, Utah, who died in 1909.

Mythic Motifs

The myths of Male Shootingway Holyway contain a relatively large number of major motifs (see Table 1), but those of the female branch of Shootingway [2] and those of the Evilway ritual have comparatively few. For example, the Evilway myths have only three fundamental motifs—*Snake Marriage*, *Coyote Transformation*, and *Bewitched by Coyote*.[3]

In the following listings the mythic motifs are italicized; the important words of the major mythic motifs are capitalized to distinguish them from the minor motifs, in which only the first word and proper nouns are capitalized.[4]

MAJOR MYTHIC MOTIFS OF MALE SHOOTINGWAY

Locale and Personnel Established. This motif, quite naturally an almost universal introduction to ceremonial myths, is covered very briefly in a few sentences in the myths of Shootingway.

Conception and Birth of Slayer Twins, *The Two Came to Their Father*, and *Monsterway* are important portions of Male Shootingway Holyway, occupying about one-fourth of the versions by Blue Eyes and Red Point and fully two-thirds of the version by Woman Singer's Son. In the version by Red Point, however, *Monsterway* is omitted. The important minor mythic motifs of these portions of the tale are outlined in Wyman (1970, pp. 52–59) under *Monsterway* (see also Wyman, 1962, p. 34). In the stories by Blue Eyes and Woman Singer's Son the Gray Big Ye'i are found playing a *Moccasin game to determine division of day and night* (see Wyman, 1965, p. 92) before they are destroyed by the *Destructive storm* (Wyman, 1970, p. 58).

Council of Holy People to Plan Action in Shootingway is for determining the future order of ceremonials and who should be in charge of each one (see Wyman, 1962, pp. 43, 64).

---

[2] Descriptions and illustrations of Female Shootingway sandpaintings may be found in Newcomb and Reichard (1937, pp. 35, 47, 49, 63, fig. 4, pls. 15, 24) and in Kluckhohn and Wyman (1940, pp. 155–168, figs. 9, 10).

[3] Spencer (1957, pp. 116–122, 205–211) has provided excellent abstracts of these.

[4] An analysis of Navaho mythology and its universal, minor, major, and unique motifs are presented in three works by Wyman (1962, pp. 29–77; 1965, pp. 65–103; 1970, pp. 39–62); and the terms used in those works to designate the mythic motifs are used here.

Shattered by Thunder (*Lightning*) appears to be a fundamental motif of the chants of the Shootingway subgroup as well as of the Windways, which may belong in this subgroup (Wyman, 1962, pp. 48, 64, 66). Moreover, it is one of the two main motifs of Flintway which, as we have seen, also is associated with Male Shootingway. It seems significant, therefore, that the only major mythic motif mentioned by Father Berard's informant (White Singer, of Chinle, Arizona) in the brief introductory paragraph to his account of ceremonial procedure in Male Shootingway's prayer-stick phase is *Shattered by Thunder* (Haile, 1947b, p. 77).

Snake Visit (*Marriage*) is the only motif (other than *Prototype Ceremonial*, virtually a universal motif) that is shared by the three Holyway and both Evilway myths. In the latter, however, this episode is a *Snake Marriage*, while in two of the Holyway stories (Blue Eyes and Woman Singer's son) it is merely a *Visit*. The *Marriage* in Red Point's story may occur in this tale because the author combined Holyway and Evilway elements in his narration (see Reichard, 1939, p. 37). The *Witch Father-in-law* motif is developed at length, however, in only one myth (by Gray Man), but the use of *Poison or overpowering tobacco* to overcome Big Snake Man occurs in the stories of Blue Eyes and Red Point as well as in the version by Gray Man. A *Snake Marriage* is a substantial part of three Navaho Windway myths (Wyman, 1962, pp. 44, 51, 75–76). *Witch Father-in-law* is a major motif

of Enemyway and is described by Wyman under *Enemyway* (1970, pp. 59–60).

Whirling Tail-feather (see No. 1, Walcott catalog) may be either the conquest of a dangerous whirling object (as in the stories of Blue Eyes and Woman Singer's Son) or a preliminary to *Pulling down Sun, Moon, and Winds* (as in the story by Red Point); along with the latter, it is one of the few unique major mythic motifs of Shootingway (Wyman, 1962, p. 54).

Visits to Supernaturals (*Journey for Knowledge and Power*). Most of the hero's adventures in nearly all ceremonial myths (or, in other words, a large part of a myth outside of the *Prototype Ceremonial(s)*) consist of visits to supernaturals in quest of knowledge and power (Spencer, 1957, p. 21; Wyman, 1962, p. 29; 1965, p. 65). The terminology of this motif as expressed here, however, is used to designate such visits as occur apart from the more complicated and fully related episodes. Usually there is a series of such visits (or perhaps several series or isolated instances) interspersed between the other major motifs (Wyman, 1962, p. 52). Some of the hero's more perilous adventures during a visit are the result of *Supernatural Injunctions Disobeyed*. Two visits, perhaps, are important enough to merit designation as independent major mythic motifs; one is to the Arrow People (in the stories of Blue Eyes and Red Point) and the other is to the home of Changing Woman (in the stories of Blue Eyes and Woman Singer's Son), where Sky People also are

TABLE 1.—*Major mythic motifs of Male Shootingway in five versions of the myth*

Major mythic motif	Author				
	Blue Eyes	Red Point	Woman Singer's Son	Gray Man	Jim Smith
Locale and Personnel Established	*1	1	1	–	1
Conception and Birth of Slayer Twins	2	2	2	–	–
The Two Came to Their Father	3	3	3	–	–
Monsterway	4	–	4	–	–
Council of Holy People to Plan Action	5	–	5	–	–
Shattered by Lightning (Thunder)	6	–	10	–	–
Snake Visit (Marriage)	7	7	6	1	2
Whirling Tail-Feather	8	4	9	–	–
Pulling down Sun, Moon, and Winds	15	5	–	–	–
Visits to Supernaturals (Journey for Knowledge and Power)	9	6	12	–	–
Captured by Thunders (Sky Visit)	10	9	7	–	–
Swallowed by Fish	11	10	8	–	–
Encounter (Trip) with Buffalos	12	12	11	–	–
Attack, Destruction, Restoration by Supernaturals	13	13	–	–	–
Coyote Transformation	–	8	–	2	3
Bewitched by Coyote	–	–	–	3	4
Prototype Ceremonial(s)	14	11	13	4	5
Hero Returns Home, Teaches Ceremonial	–	14	14	–	–

* The numerals indicate the order in which the motifs appeared in the version of each author.

encountered. Other, less-extensive visits are to Corn People (in Blue Eyes and Woman Singer's Son), to Medicine, Rock Crystal, and Water Monster People, and to Spotted Wind and Porcupine Man (in Blue Eyes), to Ant People (in Red Point): also, Holy Man and Holy Boy visit their counterparts, the Slayer Twins, in the story by Woman Singer's Son.

Captured by Thunders and *Swallowed by Fish* are interrelated episodes which are illustrated by the double sandpainting (see Nos. 10, 11, Walcott catalog). Also, these episodes appear to be fundamental motifs of Shootingway Holyway, as they occur in all versions of its myth. *Captured by Thunders* involves a *Sky Visit* with encounters with Big Thunder as well as various Sky People (Wyman, 1962, p. 50).

Encounter (Trip) with Buffalos likewise is a fundamental major motif, not only in Male Shootingway Holyway but also in Flintway, where it is one of the two main motifs of the chant (see *Shattered by Thunder*, above, and Spencer, 1957, pp. 205–208). In fact, there is nothing unique in the myth of Flintway except perhaps the emphasis on the restoration of the hero by Gila Monster. The close relationship between the Flint and Male Shooting Chants has been pointed out by several persons, and Miguelito himself said that Flintway branches off from the buffalo story of Shootingway (Haile, 1943, pp. 44, 275; Reichard, 1950, pp. 330, 332; Kluckhohn, 1960, p. 69; Wyman, 1962, p. 51).

Attack, Destruction, Restoration by Supernaturals, like *Visits to Supernaturals*, is a motif used here to designate all such episodes not extensive enough to merit separate status (Wyman, 1965, p. 98). Of course, *Shattered by Thunder* is a supernatural attack, as are *Captured by Thunders* and *Swallowed by Fish*, the battle with the buffalos, and Coyote's attack in the transformation motif, but each of these is important enough to receive a separate designation. Some of the attacking supernaturals are Bears and White Weasel (in Blue Eyes) and Ant People (in Red Point). Restoration may be accomplished by the attackers or, more often, by other supernaturals.

Coyote Transformation is almost an essential motif for Evilway ritual, as it occurs in all Evilway myths, but it is not so closely restricted to that ritual as has sometimes been said (Wyman, 1962, p. 49; 1965, pp. 65, 74). It is found in some versions of Holyway myths (Red Antway, for example) and in the myth by Red Point, although here it may be that the author was combining Holyway and Evilway episodes in one story (see, under *Snake Visit*, above) *Retaliation against Coyote* by means of *Fatal hot rock food* occurs only in the story by Jim Smith (Wyman, 1962, p. 50; 1965, p. 98).

Bewitched by Coyote follows the *Transformation* quite logically in both Evilway myths. *Retaliation against Coyote* by means of *Pursuing arrows* provides for the prototype of the Overshooting ceremony in the story by Gray Man; and in the stories of both Gray Man and Jim Smith the bewitchment is the cause of the hero's illness, which is treated by the *Prototype Ceremonials*.

Prototype Ceremonial(s), held for the hero made ill by his various misadventures, occurs in all Shootingway myths; in fact, it occurs in the myths of all ceremonials except Excessway, and the Dark Circle of Branches phase (Corral or Fire Dance) is at least mentioned in all (Wyman, 1962, p. 52). Other chants are visited and properties are received from or exchanged with them in the stories by Blue Eyes (Hail, Awl Chants) and Woman Singer's Son (Awl). The *Shock rite* occurs in the myth by Red Point; *Restoration by marking away* occurs in the stories by Blue Eyes and Gray Man; and a prototype *Sucking rite* for the effects of witchcraft is described by Gray Man. The motifs of unacceptable offerings refused four times by the prospective singers and the *Squirrel skin pouch* are elaborated upon in the story by Jim Smith (see Wyman, 1962, p. 70).

The *Hero Returns Home, Teaches Ceremonial* is a motif found only in the stories of Red Point and Woman Singer's Son; and *Hero Departs to Live with Supernaturals* and the final departure of the Holy People themselves, which form the closing episodes of practically all chantway myths, occur only in the myth told by Red Point (Wyman, 1962, p. 53).

The following motifs are not included in the table because each occurs in only one of the five myths. In the myth told by Woman Singer's Son the adventures of the Slayer Twins are preceded by the *Birth of Changing Woman* and her *Puberty Ceremonial*, themes which are elaborated upon in the myths of Blessingway (see Wyman, 1970). *Changing Woman's Departure for the West* to occupy the new home built for her by the Sun (she is persuaded to go because of intimidation by her sons and their counterparts), is developed at length in the story by Blue Eyes (Newcomb and Reichard, 1937, pp. 33–34). *The Two Returned to Their Father* for further testing, instruction, and paraphernalia is another motif in the myth related by Blue Eyes.

It may seem strange that the events which figure so importantly in the early part of the myths of Male Shootingway Holyway—the birth and rearing of the Slayer Twins, their trip to visit their father, and the slaying of the monsters—are not illustrated in the repertory of Shootingway sandpaintings, whereas most of the other major mythic motifs, in fact all the fundamental ones, are richly represented by narrative or by reminiscent designs. Except for paintings of the Slayer Twins and their counterparts and of representations of the Sun's House, which are actually substitutes for a material property, there are no known sand-paintings that could be considered illustrations of the *Conception and Birth, The Two Came to Their Father,* and *Monsterway.* In fact, the only drypaintings on record intended to illustrate the last two episodes are those for the War Prophylactic Rite recorded and published by Maud Oakes (1943; see also Wyman, 1970, p. 69). It may be that these early events are considered to be part of—or at least intimately linked to—the general-ized *Origin Myth* and that drypaintings are regarded as mainly appropriate for the portions of the legends specific for the chantway.

MYTHIC MOTIFS OF FEMALE SHOOTINGWAY

In Woman Singer's myth of Female Shootingway the major motifs are the *Separation of the Sexes* (Wyman, 1965, pp. 80–84), merely mentioned in the story; *The Emergence* (Wyman, 1965, pp. 85–87), which follows immediately; a few *Post-Emergence Events* such as *Earth drained, Badger investigates,* and *Earth Dried by Winds* (Wyman, 1965, pp. 88–90); *Locale and Personnel Established,* consisting of one short paragraph; *Shattered by Lighting;* and *Mummifying Woman.* The latter motif, which makes up a third of the story, also is important in Navaho Windway mythology (see Wyman, 1962, pp. 65–69). The myth told by Hoskinini, like that told by Woman Singer, consists mainly of the story of *Mummifying Woman,* which makes up three-fourths of the tale. That motif is followed by an *Attack by Spider Man* and *Shattered by Thunder.*

Since the *Origin Myth* or portions of it may be used as a preface to a ceremonial myth, it appears that the fundamental motifs of the Female Shootingway myth are *Shattered by Lighting* and *Mummifying Woman.* There are two forms of the chant, one said to be derived from (or taken by, according to Woman Singer) the Jicarilla Apaches and the other said to have been "preserved by the Navaho." Woman Singer's cere-monial was the latter type. Kluckhohn recorded a fragment of a legend (probably the Jicarilla form) involving a *Sky Visit* to the Turtle People and another fragment of the Female Shootingway Evilway myth (also presumably the Jicarilla form) that consisted of the *Coyote Transformation* (Kluckhohn and Wyman, 1940, pp. 45, 157).

SYMBOLISM IN SHOOTINGWAY SANDPAINTINGS

An exhaustive study of the sandpaintings of Shoot-ingway has been presented in the works of Newcomb and Reichard (1937) and Reichard (1939). These books contain color illustrations of 54 paintings and line drawings of 14 others. Reichard's (1934) semi-popular work *Spider Woman* gives a substantial account of the chant and illustrates one sandpainting in color; also, much of the material in her great two-volume work on Navaho religion (Reichard, 1950) was drawn from her studies of Shootingway, and it con-tains line drawings of three additional sandpaintings. Father Berard Haile has published two extensive works on Male Shootingway—one on prayerstick cutting (Haile, 1947b), with eight color plates of prayersticks, and the other on the myth of Male Shootingway Evilway (Haile, 1950), with a color illustration of a sandpainting.

Since these excellent works, in spite of their monu-mental character, do not present summary analyses of the sandpaintings discussed, and since most of the 28 sandpaintings in the Walcott collection are from Male Shootingway (18) and Mountain-Shootingway (4), analyses of the sandpaintings of these chants are given in the present paper. The main theme symbols and design types are listed, symbolism is discussed, published illustrations and discussions are cited, and a few examples of sandpaintings that have not been previously reproduced are illustrated.

Color, Sex, and Direction

The numerous color combinations and directional sequences of the sandpaintings of Shootingway, and the many variations and the reasons for them, have been discussed at length by Reichard (1950, chapters 12, 13). It remains to point out here only a few outstanding facts derived from an analysis of some 235 reproductions of Shootingway sandpaintings. On the whole, these facts agree substantially with Reichard's findings.

The association of color with sex is quite consistent in Shootingway sandpaintings. Black and blue are male colors, white and yellow are female (see Reichard, 1950, p. 214). The preferred male-female pair is black and white (98 instances, mostly in paired guardians), but yellow and blue also are used (in 13 paintings). Another common pair, apparently of male colors, is black and blue (24 instances mostly paired guardians). Black and yellow occur only five times, and yellow and white (both female colors) eight times. Except for four types of designs uniquely characteristic of Mountain-Shootingway, the sex of figures in Shootingway sandpaintings is not indicated by the shape of the head, as it is in some other chant-ways (Nightway, Navaho Windway, Red Antway). The Slayer Twins have round or half-round heads and so do Earth and Sky in six of eight paintings, but all other main theme symbols—Holy People, Thunders, Water Creatures, Snake People (for the most part), Buffalo, Corn, and Arrow People—have square heads regardless of sex. Reichard (1950, pp. 176–179) suggested that square-headed figures represent People (Holy People) or their intermediaries and that round heads indicate deities. The present analysis did not reveal anything which would contradict that opinion.

In 33 of 128 Shootingway sandpaintings having a radial composition (at least in part), where direction cannot be mistaken, the sunwise sequence—east, south, west, north—is white (W), blue (U), yellow (Y), black (B), which is one of the two commonest directional sequences. Predominantly, these 33 paintings are of Cosmic and Celestial Beings (Skies, 12; Sun or Moon with Pollen Boy or Ripener Girl, 11) or of Buffalo (6). The other common sequence, BUYW, which is characteristic of Navaho Windway (see Wyman, 1962, p. 285) and of other chantways, occurs in six paintings, and five of these are of the *Swallowed by Fish* portion of the double sandpainting (see No. 10, Walcott catalog), a situation which spelled danger for Holy Boy. The sequence with black in the east presages danger, and it also represents protection from danger (see Reichard, 1950, pp. 221–223; Wyman, 1962, p. 286). Likewise, three paintings with a linear sequence of BUYP (pink, substituting for white) are of the Slayer Twins or of Big Thunder, beings concerned with danger. Another sequence with black in the east, BYUP, occurs in 29 paintings; of these, 20 paintings contain Thunders and six show the Slayer Twins in action. A fourth sequence beginning with black, BUWY, is seen in 40 paintings—20 of which are of Snake People or snakes and 17 of Buffalo People or buffalo, all of these being dangerous creatures. The sunwise sequence is UBWY, in ten paintings—five of Sun, Moon, and Winds and three of their Cloud Houses, all celestial motifs. Four of the eight paintings of Arrow People show sequences beginning with blue. The Sun's jewel arrows, of course, also are celestial in origin. Attempts to depict these anthropomorphized jewel arrows result in the greatest variety of sunwise sequences in any one category, as only two of the eight paintings on record have the same sequence (BUWP). The sequences in the other six paintings are BWUY, BYWP, UWSR (S, brown; R, red), WSWR, UWVR (V, variegated), and UVWR.

In a linear composition the sunwise sequence is most commonly read from south to north, but it may be the reverse, from north to south. In eight linear paintings—of Snake People and snakes (5), Buffalo People (2), and Arrow People (1)—the south-to-north sequence is BWUY, while in eight other linear paint-

ings of Snake People it is YUWB, probably the same sunwise sequence to be read from north to south. This again is a danger sequence appropriate for these dangerous beings. Six different sequences (other than those discussed above) appear in one painting each (or two in one instance). These are not discussed here, as most likely they are the types of variation that have been treated by Reichard (1950).

The figures in 103 of 140 paintings have brown unmasked faces, but those in the remaining 37 wear the Sun's House stripes (mask or face paint): from chin to forehead—yellow, blue, black, white. Sun's House stripes are found scattered among the categories of main theme symbols, but most frequently they appear among the Holy People, Buffalo People, and Corn People, and all the Earth and Sky paintings have them (as do the Sky People paintings of Mountain-Shootingway). The figures in 68 of 157 paintings wear the pointed red feather headdress representing sunglow (Reichard, 1950, pp. 548, 603). This type of headdress is worn by Holy People in action or killing buffalo, by all Snake People, Buffalo People, and Arrow People, and by some other figures. In 67 other paintings, the head plume with the turkey-tail feather bundle (see Newcomb and Reichard, 1937, p. 45) is worn by other main theme symbols. In 22 paintings, single plumes (soft feathers) are worn by the figures, including the Slayer Twins, who also have armored headdresses of flint points and lightnings.

The direction of movement of the figures in radial compositions, indicated by position of head plumes and knee joints, is sunwise in the great majority of paintings—in 88 of 102 instances. In 58 paintings having linear compositions the movement is toward the south in 47 and toward the north in eleven. Eight of the eleven compositions having the movement toward the north are pictures of the Slayer Twins. North is the direction of evil and danger, and the powerful Twins are quite well equipped to deal with it.

Locality Centers

Of 77 paintings having radial compositions, the centers depicting the locality where the action of the picture took place represent water of some kind (a pool, lake, or the watery home of certain creatures) in 44; mountains (often the mountain home or homes of beings such as Buffalo People) in 14; houses or homes of the main theme figures in 14; and Emergence Place in five.[5] A lake may be surrounded by four mountains, the homes of Buffalo People. (Locality centers are discussed at length in Newcomb and Reichard, 1937, pp. 69–74.)

---

[5] In sandpaintings for Mountain-Shootingway the center is likely to represent the corral of the fire dance.

Quadrantal Figures

Of 87 radial compositions 36 have the four sacred domesticated plants—corn, beans, squash, and tobacco—in the quadrantal positions, as in most chantways. In 26 of the radial compositions medicine herbs are used (Medicine Herb People in one instance) as quadranted figures, and about a third of these paintings are of Buffalo People or buffalo. In five paintings four corn plants are in the quadrants, and one painting uses a corn plant and three herbs (No. 13, Walcott catalog). In Snake People or snake sandpaintings the quadrantal figures are likely to be single, pairs, or quartets of Big, straight, or crooked snakes (6 examples). In three types of design the quadrantal figures are an essential part of the composition: the Sun, Moon, and Winds in Whirling Tail Feather (4 examples); bunches of five feathers in Cloud Houses (2 examples); four hide rattles in Pollen Boy or Ripener Girl on Sun or Moon with snake guards (eclipse sandpainting; 5 examples). The quadrantal motifs are four spruce twigs in one painting and lightnings, sunbeams, and rainbows in another.

Guardians

Of 195 paintings having guardians, the encircling guardian is the Rainbow supernatural ("Goddess") in 53 and is the feathered rainbow garland in 47. Thus, these two rainbow motifs account for half of the guardians used in Shootingway sandpaintings. The mist or mirage garland occurs in another 24 paintings (of which five are snake paintings and 18 are buffalo paintings), but the anthropomorphized Mirage supernatural occurs in only three. Snakes are guardians in eight other snake paintings and in five eclipse paintings of Sun and Moon. Crooked lightnings are the guardians in 27 paintings. The Slayer Twins (in 8 instances) and Thunders (17) are likely to have black and white crooked lightning arrows guarding them (with the white member inside in most cases). Two Holy People paintings also have crooked lightnings as guardians. In 28 other paintings there are various guardians which, in most cases, are characteristic of the design type: segments of rainbow connecting the skies in Sky paintings (11) or surrounding the Sun's House (6), curved rainbow bars around snake's houses (4) or Sun and Moon (2), crooked lightnings connecting arrows for the Slayer Twins on Sun or Moon (3), and arrows guarding Arrow People (2).

Paired Guardians of the East

In 25 of the 141 sandpaintings that have small paired guardians of the eastern entrance (an optional feature) these guards are the always popular pair of Big Flies, black and white in 23 examples. Ten of these paintings are of Holy People or Slayer Twins. Ten other paintings of Holy People and Slayer Twins have Sun and Moon as paired guardians, and so do three paintings of Arrow People. Cosmic and Celestial Beings are guarded by bat and Sun's tobacco pouch in 17 paintings. Other combinations of these two symbols occur in ten paintings, bat alone (5), bat and an eagle (1), bat and Big Fly (1), and Sun's tobacco pouch and Big Fly (3). The paired guards of Thunder and Water Creature sandpaintings are most often beaver and otter (12 examples), but in one case they are a pair of crooked lightnings. Snake People and snake sandpaintings have pairs of snakes (34 examples), and usually these are crooked snakes (27), although Big, straight, or mixed snakes may be used. Two paintings of Snake People have bow-and-arrow paired guards. Buffalo People and buffalo sandpaintings have pairs of buffalo (22 examples), which usually are black and white (in 12 examples). Four of the paintings of Corn People have yellow Pollen Boy and blue Ripener Girl as guards (3), or a pair of Ripener Girls (1). One painting of Arrow People is guarded by a pair of arrows. Except for the Big Flies, which are universally used as paired eastern guardians for sandpaintings with any main theme symbols, the following motifs in Shootingway paintings are peculiarly appropriate for the main themes of the designs that they guard: Sun and Moon with Holy People and Slayer Twins, likewise powerful and important supernaturals; bat, a creature of the air, and the Sun's tobacco pouch with Cosmic and Celestial beings; beaver and otter with other beings associated with water; snakes with Snake People; buffalo with Buffalo People; and Pollen Boy and Ripener Girl, those happy symbols of fertility, with corn.

Symbolism in Small Sandpaintings

The small sandpaintings made at the cardinal points around the fireplace (beside which the ceremonial fire pokers are placed in the sweat-emetic ceremony of Shootingway) are usually of snakes (see Kluckhohn and Wyman, 1940, p. 83, figs. 11, 12; Wyman, 1962, pp. 313–314). The following are on record: BUWY Big Snakes on the first morning and BUWY crooked snakes on the third morning of Male Shootingway, Sun's House phase (chant with house); B and U crooked snakes and W and Y Big Snakes on fifth morning of Male Shootingway, Dark Circle of Branches (Corral Dance) phase; W crooked snake, U Big Snake, Y crooked snake, B Big Snake in Female Shootingway. On the second and fourth mornings of the Sun's House chant BW and W crooked lightning arrows, a WY straight sunray arrow, and a RU straight rainbow arrow were used (Reichard, 1950, fig. 29).

Four short rainbow bars indicate places for the patient's hands and knees as he kneels to drink the emetic and to vomit, and a curved rainbow bar partly encircles the sand basin which receives the vomit. Reichard (1950, pp. 721–722) stated that the small sandpaintings on which the basket of emetic was placed were cloud symbols (like those shown in Newcomb and Reichard, 1937, pl. 19), each with seven heads of Sky People emerging from it, BUYP with Sky, Water, Sun, and Summer People on successive days. In Female Shootingway a small sandpainting of four segmented clouds, BUYW, is used for the same purpose (Kluckhohn and Wyman, 1940, p. 162, fig. 13). In the Male Shootingway, Sun's House phase (discussed below), performed by Woman Singer's Son and described by Newcomb, the emetic basket was placed on a small sandpainting of the blue Sun on the first and third mornings and on one of the white Moon on the second and fourth mornings.

A drypainted trail along which the patient approaches the big hoops in the big hoop ceremony of Male Shootingway Evilway (see Wyman, 1965, pp. 56–60, 232, fig. 26) consists of pairs of black Big Snakes in front of white mountains with crooked lightning on and behind the mountains, preceding each of the big hoops from the second to the fourth in the set of five. Following the hoops are five pairs of crossed feathers. Haile (1950, pp. 192, 193, 202) and Reichard (1950, p. 715) write of big hoop trails with blue snakes and mountains being made at the south, outside the hogan, and with yellow snakes and mountains at the west, while separate small sandpaintings of Sun, Black Wind, Moon, and Yellow Wind (like those in the centers of the paintings illustrated in plates 18 and 20 in Newcomb and Reichard, 1937) are made inside the hogan on four successive days. The sweat-emetic paintings of Baskets of Arrows and the small prayer painting of spiders for Shootingway Evilway are described separately, below.

SUN'S HOUSE PHASE OF MALE SHOOTINGWAY AND ITS SANDPAINTINGS

A goodly portion of the late Gladys A. Reichard's monumental study of Navaho symbolism is devoted to explaining how shifts in symbols of various kinds, often slight and subtle, differentiate the branches and phases of a single chantway complex. In that book (Reichard, 1950, p. 324) she wrote: "Branch and phase of the Male Shooting Chant Holy are modifications of the same story and the same general procedure, with emphasis on a different symbolic theme—in one case the Sun's House. . . . Each causes some modification of other details which must be carefully learned and practiced by the chanter, but not differences of initial pattern or of myth, variations in interpretation being slight."

The major distinguishing symbol of the Sun's House phase (chant with house) of Male Shootingway is a representation of a place—the Sun's permanent home in the eastern quarter of the sky. This representation is a screen, made of rods of wood or reeds, which is a permanent property of the singer's bundle. It is made of six kinds of wood—four kinds of willow ("gray," "blue," "red," and "big"), mountain mahogany, and sumac (notes by Franc J. Newcomb, Museum of Navaho Ceremonial Art; see performance by Woman Singer's Son, below). If the screen has not been used for some time, it is refurbished with fresh paint. Fresh green fir and spruce branches are

placed around the screen, making it into a sort of booth. Wooden birds (made of yucca root, with wings of yucca leaf, in performance by Woman Singer's Son) are strung on wires above it so they can be made to "fly and sing," and wooden snakes are fixed so as to move in and out of their "houses" at the bottom of the screen (see Reichard, 1950, pp. 642, 711–713). This arrangement is set up at the west (back) side of the hogan on the fifth night of a nine-night performance, and it remains there throughout the remainder of the chant. In Plate 10 the bottom of a Sun's House screen showing the "windows" or "snakes' houses" may be seen in the background west of the double sandpainting. If the singer does not own a screen he may substitute a sandpainting of one (see No. 7, Walcott catalog, and Plate 7). "Whenever an object is lacking for a ceremony, it may be represented in sand" (Reichard, 1950, p. 116). In the first performance of a series the characterizing symbols are usually outstanding; however, in successive repetitions of the chant they need not reappear and a casual observer thus might have difficulty in classifying the ceremonial (Reichard, 1950, pp. 334, 336).

The colors on the Sun's House screen (four colored houses one above the other, in the sequence YUBW from the bottom; see No. 7, Walcott catalog) are known as Sun's House stripes. In the figure painting of the chant the stripes are applied to the face in the same order—yellow across the chin, blue across nose and cheeks, black across the eyes, and white across the forehead—giving Sun's House power to the patient; likewise, the stripes are superimposed on the natural brown of the faces of figures in the sandpaintings (see Reichard, 1950, pp. 181, 203, 645–648).

Margaret Erwin Schevill (1945, p. 4; 1947, pp. 21–22) wrote that she witnessed a performance of Mountain-Shootingway (in the country west of Oraibi and beyond Pinyon, Arizona) in which the Sun's House screen, "an important detail of the last days," was erected on the fifth day of the nine-day ceremonial. It seems likely that the Sun's House screen may be added to any kind of Shootingway, thus making it into a Sun's House phase along with whatever other phase—for example, Dark Circle of Branches—might be in progress.[6] Dr. David McAllester concurs with this opinion, stating (personal communication): "My impression is that Navahos are perfectly capable of combining almost anything with anything if they think the situation requires it—even such antithetical elements as Blessingway [see Wyman, 1970, pp. 52, 59], and Enemyway." This may be an example of flexibility in Navaho ceremonialism comparable to the flexibility in social organization that Aberle (1963) described (see discussion of the double sandpainting, following No. 11, Walcott catalog).

The Sun's House phase of Shootingway appears to be performed but rarely. Mrs. Newcomb reported in her field notes in 1939 (see below, under Walcott catalog) that she had seen it only twice; this in spite of her vast experience in witnessing Navaho ceremonials. Red Point (Miguelito) said he had used his screen only seven times. RC, McAllester's informant, said that he had not heard of anyone else who knew it, since Blue Eyes, who taught him, had died. RC, however, failed to mention SM, whom he later assisted in the latter's performance and to whom he loaned his screen for that performance. Moreover, SM's brother, from whom SM learned the chant, was still alive and participated in the performance.

The "chant with house" may be held "any time after harvest" (Newcomb, field notes), and it is not restricted to the winter months as is Mountain-Shootingway and certain other nine-night cere-

monials, such as Mountainway itself and Nightway in their full nine-night forms. This is confirmed by the fact that three of the performances listed below were held in the summer or fall months (Red Point, "summer"; Woman Singer's Son, September; SM, June). The nine-night Red Antway Holyway chant described by Wyman (1965, pp. 24, 35, 42) took place from June 12 to 21, 1963, but it is not known whether Red Antway is a recognized exception to the winter rule for nine-night chants or whether this was another instance of flexibility, since a considerable sum of money was involved. Although the performance by SM took place in June, the singer refused to discuss the texts of the songs with Dr. McAllester when he was translating them, saying that it should not be done in the summer.

Sandpaintings that were used in three actual performances and in a simulated performance are discussed below. These four performances, by different singers and covering a time span from the early 1930s to 1962, are listed below according to singer. The chant was performed in the locality of the singer's home unless otherwise indicated.

Red Point, also known as Miguelito (taught by Blue Eyes) of White Sands, six miles south of Ganado, Arizona, in "summer" 1932(?); recorder, Gladys A. Reichard. (Performance described in Reichard, 1934, pp. 144–209, and referred to many times in Reichard, 1950.)

Woman Singer's Son (taught by his mother, Woman Singer, of Two Grey Hills, New Mexico, who was a sister of Blue Eyes), of Red Rock Valley, Arizona; performance at Newcomb, New Mexico, 6–15 September 1932; recorder, Franc J. Newcomb.

RC (taught by Blue Eyes), of Lukachukai, Arizona; simulated performance at Sedona, Arizona, 17 October–3 November 1957; recorder, David P. McAllester. [RC came to Sedona, where Dr. McAllester was living, and described a performance by acting the part of a singer instructing his helpers, singing all the songs in order, and making drawings of the sandpaintings at the appropriate times, thus simulating a performance all the way through. RC's wife helped him make the drawings.]

SM (taught by his brother), of Lukachukai, Arizona, 2–10 June 1948; recorder, David P. McAllester. [RC's wife helped make the sandpaintings in SM's chant.]

The performance by Red Point was described in some detail by Reichard (1934, pp. 144–209) in her semipopular book *Spider Woman* and it is referred to many times throughout her two-volume work on Navaho religion (Reichard, 1950). Blue (Gray) Eyes, the teacher of Red Point and RC, was the author of the most extensive text we have of the myth of Male Shootingway. The story by Blue Eyes was recorded by Father Berard Haile in 1924 and was translated by Reichard; shortened forms of the translation have been published by Reichard (1934, pp. 169–179) and Newcomb and Reichard (1937, pp. 25–41). Blue Eyes was considered to be the great authority

---

[6] In the notes with the photographs taken by the late Katherine Harvey of the sandpaintings of a Sun's House performance (presumably near Kayenta, Arizona, around 1930) are the statements "Navaho fire dance" and "where we fire-danced," indicating that this ceremonial may have been a combination of the Sun's House and Dark Circle of Branches phases of Shootingway (see Plate 10).

on Shootingway, and since Woman Singer of Two Grey Hills, New Mexico, was his sister she too was considered an authority.

THE SANDPAINTINGS OF SUN'S HOUSE

Day 5: Twelve *Mixed Snake People with twelve-eared blue corn* (Red Point; Woman Singer's Son); eight *Big Snake People with twelve-eared blue corn* (RC); four *Big Snake People*, linear (SM).

Day 6: *Sky-reaching Rock*, the double sandpainting (Red Point; Woman Singer's Son; RC; SM).

Day 7: Four *Buffalo People*, linear (RC, SM); four *Buffalo People*, radial (Woman Singer's Son); *Holy People kill buffalo* (Red Point).

Day 8: *Earth and Sky* (Red Point; SM); *the Skies* with heads of Sky People (Woman Singer's Son); *Holy People quartet* (RC).

The sandpainting *Mixed Snake People with corn*, considered the key painting of the Snake group, is often used as the first painting in the Sun's House phase (Wyman, 1960, No. 33 on p. 51). In RC's first painting there are black, white, blue, and yellow (west to east) Big Snake People, one of each color on each side of the cornstalk. A painting of Snake People of some sort was the first one in all performances.

The double sandpainting (discussed at length in the Walcott catalog) was the second painting in all performances. It seems to be especially associated with the Sun's House phase, although it has been seen in Mountain-Shootingway (as has the Sun's House screen, according to Schevill, 1945).

In all performances the third sandpainting involved buffalo or Buffalo People. SM said that the painting used on the seventh day could be any Holy Young Man (Holy People) or any buffalo painting and that the Holy People Quartet would be used if the patient's olivella shell token needed renewing. In RC's painting streaks of sand finely scattered between the figures represent mirage. RC described another painting that could be used: a radial composition with pairs of Buffalo People, black and white at east and west (black north), blue and yellow at south and north, with "mirage" between them. This description reminds us of a painting in the Walcott collection (No. 14), one illustrated in Newcomb and Reichard (1937, pl. 28), and a similar one in the Bush collection.

There was greater variety on the last day in the four performances. According to SM, the last sandpainting could be chosen by the patient, and in his chant the patient chose *Earth and Sky*. The painting was unusual in that the paired guardians of the east were Pollen Boy and Ripener Girl, whereas they usually are bat and Sun's tobacco pouch (as in five of seven recorded paintings having paired guards). SM said that a painting of *Corn People with Pollen Boy and Ripener Girl* could be used.

Reichard (1950, p. 204) told of a variety of Sun's House phase called "dotted body." This variation was distinguished by the encircling guardian of sandpaintings being Mirage, a figure much like the usual Rainbow but having a body of varicolored dots which Red Point said represent all the precious stones.

Grinding Herbs for Infusion Specific

The sandpainting ceremony of the fifth day of SM's chant was over by midmorning, and at about 11:00 A.M. a special ceremony was added to grind the herbs for the chant's specific medicine (called infusion specific by Kluckhohn and Wyman, 1940, p. 51). A version of the *Grinding snakes* sandpainting was made; it had four snakes with a black square over them, so that only their heads and tails protruded. A cloth was placed over the sandpainting and a metate (grinding stone) was placed on it. On the metate were painted a black (outside) and white crooked lightning at the east, a yellow and white crooked sunbeam(?) at the south, a red and blue straight lightning arrow at the west, and a rainbow bar at the north. Two short wooden snakes were laid in line on each side of the metate, with their heads pointing east, blue (east) and black crooked snakes at the south, yellow and white straight snakes at the north. The mano (hand stone) was painted with two short rainbow bars ("sundogs") where it was to be grasped by the grinder. A prepubescent girl (it is ritually important that the girl be a virgin) started the grinding, and then various people took turns at it. Half of the ground medicine was mixed with red ochre.

Reichard noted that the sandpainting of the *Grinding snakes* is "the most precious of all sandpaintings" and is rarely used. She reported that large quantities of herbs are gathered and prepared on this painting, and this medicine is cherished and used sparingly since it might be many years before another supply is made. Also, she remarked that the somewhat similar painting of the *Emergence of Medicine People* might refer to the Sun's gift of medicine to his children. (Reichard, 1939, pp. 44, 54, pl. 15, fig. 3.)

Shock Rite

On the fifth night a sandpainting was made in front of the Sun's House screen for the shock rite (see Wyman, 1965, pp. 45, 56–58). In the performance by Woman Singer's Son it was of *White Big Snake* (for a female patient), in that by RC it was *Black Big Snake* (for a male patient), and in that by SM it was black *Coiled (Endless) snake*, with twelve coils.

Small Sandpaintings for the Sweat-Emetic Ceremony

The small sandpaintings made around the fireplace to go with the pokers and those for the emetic basket and vomit basin have been described above. In the performance by Woman Singer's Son the poker paintings were four Big Snakes, headed away from the fire on the fourth day (last ceremony). In RC's performance they were Big Snakes on the first day; crooked lightning, sunray, and rainbow arrows on the second and fourth days; and crooked (rattle) snakes on the third day. Sand of the color of the snake was finely sprinkled around the snake. This sand represented its home, and a red dot on its head meant it was poisonous. In the performance by Red Point the small sandpainting for the emetic basket was a cloud symbol with seven heads of Sky People emerging from it, a different color on each day; for Woman Singer's Son, it was Sun on the first and third days and Moon on the second and fourth days. The paintings around the patient's sandbasin were the usual curved rainbow bar and four short bars for hands and knees (see Kluckhohn and Wyman, 1940, pp. 83, 84, 121).

REPRODUCTIONS OF SHOOTINGWAY SANDPAINTINGS

More reproductions of Shootingway sandpaintings have been collected than for any other chantway. A total of 225 paintings (including examples from all but one of the major collections) for Male or Female Shootingway performed according to Holyway ritual were studied for the following analysis.[7] The collection data for the reproductions in various collections that were used in the analysis are given in Table 2. Besides these 225 reproductions there are numerous copies of some of the same paintings in various collections. This does not mean, however, that there are 225 different designs. The difficulty of deciding how many of the designs in a given collection should be considered different from one another has been discussed before (Wyman, 1962, p. 281). Moreover, many of the paintings are slightly different versions of the same design. Nine general catagories of main theme symbols are represented among the 225 paintings, and within these there are 18 or 22 types of main themes, depending on the point of view. Then there are about 56 types of design made up of these symbols. All of these are listed in Table 3.

Almost twice as many paintings are on record for Shootingway than there are for its nearest competitor, Navaho Windway, for which some 133 paintings are in collections (see Wyman, 1962, p. 279). Next in numbers are Nightway, Plumeway, Red Antway Beautyway, and Mountainway, with around 60 to 70 paintings each, and Big Starway and the Blessingway drypaintings with about 50 apiece. Beadway has around 35, Hailway around 26, and all the other chantways from nine to 18 apiece, with only three for the extinct Awlway and four for Earthway, also an extinct chant. Moreover, Shootingway exhibits a much greater variety of symbolism in its sandpaintings than does any other chantway.

Of the three types of composition used in sandpaintings, *radial* leads with 128 examples (main theme symbols cardinally oriented in a Greek cross and subsidiary symbols in the quadrants around a locality center), *linear* is next with 56 example (symbols in a row or rows), and *extended center* (enlarged central motif filling the design) has 41 examples. Of the 13 paintings recorded for Male Shootingway Evilway, six have a radial composition and another six show a composition which is essentially an extended center but with a radial arrangement of some symbols (see *Slayer Twins within Mountains*, below); only one is linear. Of the 18 paintings for Mountain-Shootingway the composition is radial in eight, linear in five, and extended center in five.

Symbols and Designs in Shootingway Sandpaintings

Since the main theme symbols and design types of Shootingway sandpaintings have, with one or two exceptions, been thoroughly described, discussed, and in most instances illustrated by Reichard in her several publications on the chant, only citations for published illustrations and discussions are given in the following list.

---

[7] The two Shootingway paintings in the Oakes collection—one of Thunders and the other of buffalo—were not available for study. Most of the reproductions in the Newcomb collection also were unavailable as they were in storage. The analyses presented in this section are of 225 reproductions of sandpaintings for Male and Female Shootingway performed according to Holyway ritual but excluding those specifically designated for the Dark Circle of Branches phase; that is, for Mountain-Shootingway. Reproductions of sandpaintings of Mountain-Shootingway and of Male Shootingway Evilway are treated separately, below.

In this list of main theme symbols and designs (as well as in the similiar lists for sandpaintings of Male Shootingway Evilway and of Mountain-Shootingway, which follow) information is presented in the following order: design type (italicized); type of composition; the symbols presented; references to published descriptions and illustrations (italicized); and explanatory remarks, if any,

PEOPLE

Holy People

Holy People quartet. Linear. Holy Man, Holy Woman, Holy Boy, Holy Girl (south to north). References: Newcomb and Reichard, 1937, pp. 45–47, *pl. 14;* Reichard, 1939, pp. 15, 38–42, 60–61, 66–67; Wyman. 1960, pp. 39–40.

Holy People guarded by Slayer Twins. Linear. Holy Man or Holy Woman in center, flanked by flint-armored Monster Slayer

TABLE 2.—*Reproductions of Shootingway sandpaintings*

Collection	Collector or recorder	Singer	Locality *	Date	Number
Walcott (18)	Matthew Murphy	Big Lefthanded	Tuba City	1905–1912	18
Huckel (48)	Sam E. Day, Jr.	Various singers (see Wyman, 1960)	Chinle	1902–1904	18
	Sam E. Day, Jr.	White Singer	St. Michaels	1923	4
	Herman Schweizer	Miguelito	Near Ganado	1924	26
Wetherill (6)	Louisa Wetherill	Sam Chief	Oljeto, Utah	1910–1918	6
Haile (25)	Father Berard Haile	Gray Man	Chinle Wash	1934	19
		Late Cane's Son	Saunders	1908	4
		Blue Eyes	Lukachukai	—	1
		Unknown	—	—	1
MNCA (32)	Laura Armer	Massive One	Black Mountain	1929	5
	Franc Newcomb	Big Lefthanded's Sons	Kayenta	Before 1930	4
	Franc Newcomb	Various singers†	Newcomb, N. Mex.	Before 1930	15
	Mary Wheelwright	Hastin Begay	Chinle	1947	1
	David McAllester	RC	Lukachukai	1957	7
Bush (47)	Franc Newcomb	Miguelito	Near Ganado	Before 1937	3
	Franc Newcomb	Various singers‡	Newcomb, N. Mex.	Before 1937	10
	Franc Newcomb	Not recorded	—	Before 1937	34
Newcomb (4)	Franc Newcomb	Various singers	Newcomb, N. Mex.	Before 1930	4
Reichard (16)	Franc Newcomb	Various singers	Newcomb, N. Mex.	Before 1937	14
	Ramon Hubbell	Miguelito	Near Ganado	About 1930	2
Ganado (5)	Ramon Hubbell	Miguelito	Near Ganado	About 1930	5
Stockholm (6)	Nils Hogner	Miguelito	Near Ganado	1929–1930	6
Formerly Hubbell (Six photos in MNCA)	Ramon Hubbell	Miguelito	Near Ganado	About 1930	6
MNM (4)	Bertha Dutton	Sam Tilden	Canyon de Chelly	1940	4
		MOUNTAIN-SHOOTINGWAY			
Walcott (4)	Matthew Murphy	Big Lefthanded	Tuba City	1905–1912	4
Huckel (2)	Sam E. Day, Jr.	Speech Man	Chinle	1904	1
	Herman Schweizer	Miguelito	Near Ganado	1924	1
Haile (2)	Father Berard	Gray Man	Chinle Wash	1934	2
MNCA (5)	Laura Armer	Massive One	Black Mountain	1929	4
	Franc Newcomb	Miguelito(?)	White Cone	—	1
MNM (4)	Bertha Dutton	Sam Tilden	Canyon de Chelly	1940	4
		SHOOTINGWAY-EVILWAY			
Haile (2)	Father Berard	Unknown	—	—	2
MNCA (10)	Franc Newcomb	Not recorded	Ganado and Dinnehotso	Before 1933	10
Reichard (1)	Franc Newcomb	James Smith	Ganado	In 1930s	1

NOTE: This table includes only reproductions of sandpaintings painted or drawn on paper, cardboard, or cloth by various white or Navaho recorders and preserved in the museums or collections indicated, and six photographs (former Hubbell). Numerous other sources were used, however, in the analysis of Shootingway sandpaintings presented in this book, such as published illustrations of sandpaintings, tapestries made by Lefthanded and his nieces, actual examples in sand, and numerous copies of those listed in the table.

* Unless otherwise noted all localities are in Arizona.
† Blue Eyes, Blue Eyes' Nephew, Dudley, Dudley and Galison, Little Big-reed, Hastin Gani.
‡ Galison, Little Big-reed, Shooting Chanter, Navaho Frank.

(south) and Born-for-Water (north). References: Newcomb and Reichard, 1937, pp. 47–49; Reichard, 1939, pp. 40–41, *pl. 10;* Wyman, 1960, p. 40.

Holy People guarded by Ye'i. Linear. Holy Boy or Holy Girl in center, flanked by Talking God (south) and Calling God (north). References: Reichard, 1939, p. 61, *pl. 20;* Wyman, 1960, p. 41.

Holy People in Action

Whirling Tail Feathers. See No. 1, Walcott catalog.
Taking down the Sun. Radial. Holy Man, Holy Boy, Holy Woman, Holy Girl; Sun, Black Wind, Moon, Yellow Wind in quadrants. Reference: Reichard, 1939, pp. 47–48, *fig. 5.*

Emergence of Medicine People. Radial. The Holy People (single or pairs); heads of twelve Medicine People emerging from each side of square black center (Emergence Place). References: Reichard, 1939, pp. 44–45, *fig. 3;* Wyman, 1960, p. 44.

Slayer Twins
(Used in Male and in Female Shootingway)

Single, pair, or *quartet of Slayer Twins.* Linear. Monster Slayer, Born-for-Water, Changing Grandchild, Reared-in-the-Earth; flint-armored. References: Newcomb and Reichard, 1937, pp. 34, 47–49, *pl. 16, fig. 4;* Reichard, 1939, pp. 40–41, 65; Kluckhohn and Wyman, 1940, pp. 164, 167–168, *figs. 9, 10;* Wyman, 1960, pp. 41–42, *fig. 14* (cf. Wheelwright, 1949, p. 157).

TABLE 3.—*Main theme symbols and designs of Shootingway Holyway sandpaintings*

PEOPLE

HOLY PEOPLE		*9(3)
Holy People quartet	5(1)	
guarded by Slayer Twins	2(1)	
guarded by Ye'i	2(1)	
HOLY PEOPLE IN ACTION		9(2)
Whirling Tail Feathers	5(2)	
Taking down the Sun	1	
Emergence of Medicine People	3	
SLAYER TWINS		9(1)
single	2	
pair	2(1)	
quartet	5	
SLAYER TWINS ON THE SON OR MOON		8(4)
Monster Slayer on Sun	5(2)	
Born-for-Water on Moon	3(2)	
SLAYER TWINS IN ACTION		7(4)
with house and/or mountains		

COSMIC AND CELESTIAL BEINGS

EARTH AND SKY		10
THE SKIES		17(5)
trapezoid form	10(4)	
rectangle form	2	
cloud symbol form	5(1)	
CLOUD HOUSES		3
SUN, MOON AND WINDS		6
SUN OR MOON WITH POLLEN BOY OR RIPENER GIRL		14(1)
Pollen Boy on Sun	1	
with rays	3	
with lightnings	1	
with snake guards (eclipse)	4(1)	
Ripener Girl on Moon		
with rays	3	
with lightnings	1	
with snake guards (eclipse)	1	
SUN'S HOUSE		8(2)
sandpainting	2	
with Sky People on clouds	5(2)	
four Sun's Houses with Slayer Twins	1	

THUNDERS AND WATER CREATURES

THUNDERS		11(3)
radial	4(1)	
Big Thunder	1(1)	
Holy Man captured by Thunders	6(1)	
WATER CREATURES		2(1)
Fish People	1(1)	
Water Monsters	1	
THUNDERS AND WATER CREATURES		15(1)
radial	5	
Sky-reaching Rock (double sandpainting)	10(1)	

RAINBOW PEOPLE 2

Rainbow's house	1	
Whirling Rainbows	1	

SNAKE PEOPLE AND SNAKES

SNAKE PEOPLE		28(4)
Big Snake People	9(2)	
Straight Snake People	4	
Crooked Snake People	8	
mixed Snake People	7(2)	
SNAKES		29(3)
Big Snakes	4	
Big Snake—shock rite	4(1)	
crooked snakes	1	
mixed snakes	4	
coiled (Endless) snakes	5(1)	
whirling snakes	1	
snakes on house	4	
grinding snakes	6(1)	

BUFFALO PEOPLE AND BUFFALO

BUFFALO PEOPLE		5
BUFFALO		19(6)
radial	8(2)	
Holy People kill buffalo	11(4)	
KINGBIRD PEOPLE		1
CORN PEOPLE		7(1)
linear	3(1)	
with Pollen Boy and Ripener	4	
ARROW PEOPLE		8(3)
BASKETS		4

*Number of reproductions of sandpaintings having the symbol. Numerals in parentheses represent the number of copies of the same design in collections.

Slayer Twins on Sun or Moon
(Used exclusively in Female Shootingway)

Monster Slayer on Sun. Extended center. With or without guardians. References: Newcomb and Reichard, 1937, p. 47, *pl. 15;* Wyman, 1952, *fig. 8;* 1960, p. 43.

Slayer Twins in Action

Slayer Twins with house and/or mountains. Radial. Slayer Twin quartet around house or mountain(s), or both. References: Newcomb and Reichard, 1937, *pl. 17;* Reichard, 1939, *pls. 17–19;* also, see No. 2, Walcott catalog.

COSMIC AND CELESTIAL BEINGS

Earth and Sky

See No. 3, Walcott catalog.

The Skies

Trapezoid form. See No. 4, Walcott catalog.
Rectangle form. Radial. References: Mullen, 1964, *p. 19 (color);* Tanner, 1964, pp. 6–19, *illustration on p. 15 (color).* A version of this design was collected by Laura A. Armer at Black Mountain, Arizona, in 1929; it was said to be used in Female Shootingway.
Cloud symbol form. Radial. With or without Sky People (standing on cloud or heads emerging from cloud). References: Newcomb and Reichard, 1937, pp. 57–59, *pl. 18;* Reichard, 1939, pp. 43–44, *fig. 2;* Wyman, 1960, p. 45. A cloud symbol with seven heads of Sky People emerging from it may be used separately (Sky, Sun, Water, or Summer People) as a prayer painting in the early morning of the Sun's House or the Prayerstick phase of Male Shootingway (see Newcomb and Reichard, 1937, p. 59, *pl. 19).*

Cloud Houses

See Nos. 5 and 6, Walcott catalog.

Sun, Moon, and Winds

Radial. Blue Sun, Black Wind, white Moon, Yellow Wind; with or without Sun's House stripe masks. References: Tozzer, 1909, pp. 331–332, *pl. 5;* Coolidge and Coolidge, 1930, pp. 227–229, *illustration on p. 228;* Newcomb, 1931, *p. 9 (illustration);* Newcomb and Reichard, 1937, pp. 57–58, *fig. 8;* MD Medical News Magazine, 1966, vol. 10, *p. 184 (illustration).*

Sun or Moon with Pollen Boy or Ripener Girl

Pollen Boy on Sun with rays or lightnings. Extended center. References: Newcomb and Reichard, 1937, p. 56, *pl. 2B;* Wheelwright, 1946a, *p. 171 (Hailway, illustration);* Wyman, 1952, p. 37; 1962, pp. 300–302, *fig. 31 (Navaho Windway).*
Ripener Girl on Moon with rays or lightnings. References: Newcomb and Reichard, 1937, *pl. 2D;* Wheelwright, 1946a, *p. 173 (Hailway; illustration).*
Pollen Boy on Sun or Ripener Girl on Moon with two snake guardians (eclipse sandpainting). References: Newcomb and Reichard, 1937, p. 56, *pl. 11;* Reichard, 1939, pp. 48–49; Boyd, 1953, *p. 86 (color illustration).*

Sun's House

See No. 7, Walcott catalog.
Sun's House with Sky People on clouds. Extended center and radial. Four cloud symbols around Sun's House with five or seven heads of Sky People emerging from each (the cloud with Sky People's heads may be used separately as a prayer painting; see *The Skies).* References: Newcomb and Reichard, 1937, *pl. 19;* Reichard, 1934, *p. 28 (illustration).*
Sun's Houses with Slayer Twins. Radial. The Slayer Twins, accompanied by black Big Fly and brown otter, are surrounded by four sets of Sun's House screens. This unique painting (in the Bush collection) is the most elaborate Sun's House sandpainting (see Plate 36). It is described in the myth of Male Shootingway dictated to Father Berard Haile in 1924 by Blue (Gray) Eyes of Lukachukai, Arizona (MS. in MNA). According to this myth the painting was shown to the Slayer Twins by the Sun when *The Two Returned to Their Father.* Monster Slayer (Holy Man) said: "It was made with us lying in the center and four houses stood there made with cloud figures extending above on the top of which were small birds. Below were four square openings from which figures could be seen, and below these snake heads appeared." Holy Man is at the north accompanied by Big Fly and otter, and Holy Boy is at the south with five arrow points and five medicines suspended from his neck and with an arrow point and five medicines in his hands. Both Holy Man and Holy Boy have a bow and arrow and Sun's House face stripes.

THUNDERS AND WATER CREATURES

Thunders

Radial. Four Thunders around their home (lake). References: Newcomb and Reichard, 1937, pp. 39, 61–62, *pls. 30, 31;* Reichard, 1939, p. 57; Watkins, 1943, *fig. 18* (Navaho Windway); Wheelwright, 1946a, *p. 165* (Hailway, *illustration);* Wyman, 1952, *fig. 39* (Plumeway); 1960, p. 48.
Big Thunder. Extended center. A single Black Big Thunder with four Thunders on its body. References: Reichard, 1939, pp. 58–60, *frontispiece, fig. 7;* Wyman, 1957, *pl. 15* (Beautyway); 1960, p. 48.
Holy Man captured by Thunders. See No. 9, Walcott catalog.

Water Creatures

Fish People. See No. 8, Walcott catalog.
Water Monsters. Radial. Four Water Monsters around lake. Reference: Newcomb and Reichard, 1937, p. 62, *pl. 32.*

Thunders and Water Creatures

Radial. Water Monster, Thunder, Water Horse, in sets of three or singly around lake. References: Newcomb and Reichard, 1937, pp. 39, 61–62, 72, *pls. 29, 33;* Reichard, 1939, pp. 62–64, *fig. 8;* 1950, p. 706, *fig. 24;* Wyman, 1960, p. 49.
Sky-reaching Rock (double sandpainting). See Nos. 10 and 11, Walcott catalog.

RAINBOW PEOPLE

Rainbow's house. Linear. Rectangular block of twelve Rainbow bodies with six heads and legs. Reference: Wyman, 1962, pp. 302–304, *fig. 41 (line),* cf. *figs. 39, 40, 42* (Navaho Windway).
Whirling Rainbows. Radial. Four curved Rainbow People around lake. References: Wyman, 1957, p. 177, *pl. 11* (Beautyway); 1962, pp. 304–305, *figs. 43B (line), 44 (color;* Navaho Windway).

SNAKE PEOPLE AND SNAKES

Snake People

Big Snake People. Linear. Pair or quartet. References: Newcomb, 1936, *p. 25 (illustration);* Newcomb and Reichard, 1937, pp. 54, 85, *pl. 6;* Wyman, 1957, p. 167, *fig. 1* (Beautyway).

Big Snake People with twelve-eared corn. Linear. Pairs of Big Snake People on each side of twelve-eared cornstalk. References: Newcomb and Reichard, 1937, *pl. 3*; Wyman and Newcomb, 1962, pp. 47–50.

Big Snake People. Radial. See No. 12, Walcott catalog.

Straight Snake People. Linear (quartet) or radial (pairs). References: Newcomb and Reichard, 1937, p. 72, *pl. 7* (cf. Reichard, 1939, p. 55, *pl. 14*); Wyman, 1952, p. 36; 1960, p. 52.

Crooked Snake People. Linear (quartet) or radial (single or quartets). References: Newcomb and Reichard, 1937, pp. 50, 52–54, 70, *pls. 4, 5;* Reichard, 1939, p. 53; Wyman, 1960, pp. 52, 53.

Mixed Snake People. Linear. Twelve or 24 Snake People arranged in sets of Straight, Crooked, and Big Snake People on each side of twelve-eared corn. References: Newcomb and Reichard, 1937, pp. 54, 67, *pl. 3;* Reichard, 1939, p. 53; Wyman, 1960, pp. 51–52.

Mixed Snake People. Radial. See No. 13, Walcott catalog.

Snakes

Big Snakes. Linear (quartet) or radial (pairs). References: Newcomb and Reichard, 1937, p. 53; Reichard, 1939, p. 51; Wyman, 1957, pp. 167–169, 188, *fig. 1 (line)*, *pl. 2 (color; Beautyway)*; 1962, pp. 297–298, *figs. 24A–C, 25* (Navaho Windway).

Big Snake—shock rite. Extended center. Black or White Big Snake curved around a black ground bearing four bear tracks. References: Reichard, 1939, p. 66, *pl. 21* (cf. Wyman, 1965, *figs. 20–25*, Red Antway); Kluckhohn and Wyman, 1940, p. 73; Wyman, 1960, p. 55; 1965, pp. 56–58. In a painting by Red Point (Miguelito) once owned by the late Ramon Hubbell, Ganado, Arizona (present location of painting unknown), Holy Young Man and the Bear, who are represented by costumed impersonators in the rite in practice (see Wyman, 1965, p. 57), are shown east of the black ground (see Plate 37, herein). White Big Snake is used for a female patient.

Crooked snakes. Linear (quartet). References: Newcomb and Reichard, 1937, pp. 52–53; Reichard, 1939, p. 52; Wyman, 1957, p. 167; 1960, p. 54; 1962, p. 298, *figs. 24E, F* (Navaho Windway).

Mixed snakes. Linear. Three quartets; pair pierced by arrows; three quartets of Big, crooked, and straight snakes on each side of 24-eared corn. Reference: Newcomb and Reichard, 1937, pp. 53, 74, *fig. 6.*

Coiled (Endless) snakes. Radial. Large Endless (coiled) Snake in center, four smaller coiled snakes in cardinal positions; straight snake guardian(s). References: Newcomb and Reichard, 1937, pp. 13, 53, 78, *pls. 12, 13;* Reichard, 1939, p. 54; Wyman, 1957, pp. 168, 176, *fig. 3 (line)*, *pl. 6 (color; Beautyway)*; 1960, p. 55; 1962, pp. 299–300, *fig. 30 (halftone; Navaho Windway).*

Whirling snakes. Radial. Four curved snakes around "Whirling Mountain"; straight snake guardian. Reference: Newcomb and Reichard, 1937, pp. 53, 78, *pl. 10.*

Snakes on house. Extended center. Pair of crooked snakes crossed on circular house; prayer painting. References: Newcomb and Reichard, 1937, p. 56, *pl. 2A;* Wyman, 1957, pp. 168, 188, *fig. 3 (line)*, *pl. 3 (color; Beautyway).*

Grinding snakes (crooked snakes move their home). Radial. Pairs or quartets of Crooked, Straight, or Mixed Snake People around square or rectangular black center (metate) with blue or white rectangle (mano) on it; heads and tails of twelve (or eight) snakes emerging from each side. References: Coolidge and Coolidge, 1930, pp. 231–233, *frontispiece (halftone)*; Newcomb and Reichard, 1937, p. 54, *pl. 9;* Reichard, 1939, p. 54, *pl. 15;* Wyman, 1960, pp. 53–54.

BUFFALO PEOPLE AND BUFFALO

Buffalo People

Linear and radial. See No. 14, Walcott catalog.

Buffalo

Radial. See No. 15, Walcott catalog. Quartets of buffalo around a lake may be used in Female Shootingway.

Holy People kill buffalo. See No. 16, Walcott catalog.

KINGBIRD PEOPLE

Radial. Blue Kingbird (Titmouse) People around blue Sun; crooked lightning and arrow guardian. This unique painting (in MNCA) is used in Female Shootingway. References: Plate 38, herein; Newcomb and Reichard, 1937, p. 65. The identity of the Bird People in this sandpainting is uncertain because the painting is labeled "titmouse," but the Navaho name given for the birds has been identified by various authors as the name for the western kingbird, the cedar waxwing, and the plain or bridled titmouse. The design is unusual in having the eastern opening in the southeast.

CORN PEOPLE

Linear. See No. 17, Walcott catalog.

Corn People with Pollen Boy and Ripener Girl. Linear and radial. References: Newcomb and Reichard, 1937, *fig. 10, pl. 22;* also, see No. 17 of Walcott catalog herein (cf. Wyman and Bailey, 1964, pp. 29, 131–132, 141–144, *pl. 3*).

ARROW PEOPLE

Linear (quartet). Reference: Reichard, 1939, *pl. 11.*

Radial. See No. 18, Walcott catalog.

BASKETS

Extended center. Blue Sun's, White Moon's, Black Wind's, or Yellow Wind's basket (circle), each surrounded by twelve feathers; prayer painting. Reference: Newcomb and Reichard, 1937, p. 56, pl. *2C.*

SUMMARY OF SYMBOLISM

Shootingway sandpaintings have more main theme symbols and design types which are peculiar to the chantway than have those of any other ceremonial. Among the main theme symbols belonging exclusively to Shootingway are Sky People (Mountain-Shootingway); the Skies with trapezoid, rectangular, or cloud symbol form; cloud houses; Sun and Moon together with Black and Yellow Wind; Sun's house; Buffalo People and buffalo; Kingbird People (in Female Shootingway); Arrow People; baskets. In addition, numerous main theme symbols that are shared with other chantways are found in design types peculiar to Shootingway, such as Holy People or Slayer Twins involved in various kinds of actions (see Table 3), Slayer Twins on Sun or Moon (in Female Shootingway), Pollen Boy or Ripener Girl on Sun or Moon with snake guards, the double sandpainting (Sky-reaching Rock), the shock rite sandpainting with Big Snake, grinding snakes, Corn People with Pollen Boy and Ripener Girl.

Most of the reproductions of Shootingway sandpaintings in collections are from the male branch. The female branch employs relatively few main theme symbols and designs—the Slayer Twins, singly, in pairs, or quartets (used for both male and female branches); the Slayer Twins on Sun or Moon (used exclusively in Female Shootingway); quartets of buffalo around a lake (used for both branches); and the unique painting of Kingbird or Titmouse People (Plate 38). Reichard (Newcomb and Reichard, 1937, p. 47) said that Female Shootingway differs from the male branch "in emphasizing the birth and rearing of the Twins as against their dangerous exploits." Other symbols that have been attributed to Female Shootingway in scattered notes from various sources are the Skies, Thunders, Cloud People, Big Fly, Snake People and Snakes, Water Monster, and curved rainbows, but without further evidence these attributions should be regarded only as suggestive clues.

Twenty-one main theme symbols and design types of Shootingway sandpaintings are shared with the drypaintings of Blessingway and all other chantways except Eagleway and Awlway (see Table 4). These symbols are in eleven groups: Slayer Twins, Earth and Sky, Pollen Boy or Ripener Girl on Sun or Moon, Thunders, Water Creatures, Rainbow People, Snake People, snakes, Corn People, corn, and mountains. Of these, the Thunders appear most often in other chants. The number of ceremonials that share any given symbol and the number of symbols found in the paintings of any given ceremonial as well as in Shootingway may be derived from Table 4.

The following correspondences are not indicated in the table. Among the drypaintings for the War Prophylactic Rite illustrated by Oakes (1943), the Slayer Twins, single Corn People, and mountains appear as main themes and Thunders and Big Snakes as guardians of the Sun's house. Thunders are the

TABLE 4.—*Symbols of Shootingway sandpaintings shared with other ceremonials*

Shootingway symbol	Other ceremonials													
	Bless-ing	Hail	Water	Red Ant	Big Star	Moun-tain	Beauty	Night	Plume	Navaho Wind	Chiri-cahua Wind	Bead	Earth	Up-ward-Reach-ing
Slayer Twins	X	X			X									X
Earth and Sky	S*				X	X			S				X	
Pollen Boy on Sun	X				X		X		X	X	X			
Ripener Girl on Moon							X		X	X	X			
Thunders (radial)		X			X		X		X	X				
Big Thunder							X		X					
Water Creatures			X				X		X					
Thunder(s) and Water Creatures							X		X					
Whirling (curved) Rainbow People						X	X	X	X	X				
Snake People										X		X		
Big Snake					X	G	X			X	G	X		X
Straight Snakes					X	X	X			X				
Crooked Snakes					X	X	X			X		X		
Coiled (Endless) Snakes					G†		X			X				
Snakes with House							X			X				
Sun, Moon Clothed in Snakes							X			X				
Corn People	X			X										
Corn Plants	X			X			X		X					
Mountains	X	X			X			X						
No. symbols shared	6	3	1	2	9	5	14	2	9	11	2	3	1	2

* S: Earth or Sky separately.

† G: As guardian only.

quadrantal figures in a painting for Big Godway, in another for Coyoteway, and in the Gila Monster painting of Hand-trembling Evilway. Portions of the Earth or of the Sky sandpainting of Big Starway may be used in divination rites (see Wyman and Newcomb, 1963, pp. 21–23). A version of Holy Man captured by Thunders is one of the sandpaintings for Hailway in the Oakes collection (No. 51). Rainbow's House, which appears in eight paintings of Navaho Windway, occurs in only one Male Shootingway painting (No. 25 in the Haile collection; Wyman, 1962, fig. 41, cf. figs. 39, 40, 42, and pp. 302–303).

The chantways sharing the largest number of symbols with Shootingway are Beautyway (14), Navaho Windway (11), and Big Starway (9). The first two, like Shootingway, place great emphasis on snakes, and in Big Starway snakes are frequently combined with stars. Earth or Sky appear separately as main theme symbols for several ceremonials (see Table 4). The water creatures of a Beautyway painting are frogs (Wyman, 1957, pl. 14). The snakes of Mountainway sandpaintings are main theme symbols and also guardians in the design representing the Home of Bear and Snake (Matthews, 1887, pl. 15). The Corn People of the Blessingway drypaintings are a single figure in one instance and a pair of twelve-eared Corn People in the other. In the Navaho Windway paintings of snakes with their house, the snakes are not crossed on the house as in the Shootingway design but are arranged in cardinal positions around it (Wyman, 1962, fig. 26). Moun-

tains are main theme symbols in Male Shootingway Evilway sandpaintings (Wyman, 1967a, fig. 1) and in sandpaintings of five other ceremonials. Sun or Moon clothed in snakes, a Mountain-Shootingway theme, is found also in Beautyway and Navaho Windway sandpaintings.

Of course numerous symbols that appear as subsidiary figures in the quadrants of radial compositions or in other positions—Sun and Moon, the four sacred plants, medicine herbs and Medicine Herb People, corn plants, bows and arrows, lightnings, and the like, and the various symbols serving as paired guardians of the east—are found both in the sandpaintings of Shootingway and in those of many if not most other ceremonials.

Among a number of sunwise color sequences (east, south, west, north), the following predominate, WUYB (33), BUWY (40), BYUP (29), UBWY (10), BUYW (6). The linear sunwise sequence is most commonly from south to north but it may be the reverse. Black and blue are male colors, white and yellow are female, and the preferred male-female pair is black and white, but other pairs occur. In figures of People, square heads predominate regardless of sex, faces are usually brown (103) but Sun's House stripes are frequent (37) and so is the pointed red feather headdress characteristic of the chantway (68). The direction of movement of the figures in radial compositions is sunwise in the majority of paintings, and in linear compositions it is towards the south.

Mountain-Shootingway Sandpaintings

The performance popularly called a Fire Dance is a spectacular all-night exhibition of various acts by teams representing various chantways—each team putting on a specialty of its chant, and culminating in the Fire Dance proper, in which nearly naked, clay-daubed dancers run about brandishing torches of cedar bark amid showers of sparks. The whole is like a great sacred vaudeville show—and provides the climax on the final night of a nine-night ceremonial. A chant that includes this feature must last nine nights. The performance is carried out in a great circle or "corral" of evergreen branches, hence the other popular name, Corral Dance, and the formal Navaho designation, Dark Circle of Branches. The Fire Dance is usually associated with a Mountain Chant, but other ceremonials may have this phase, although some, such as Hailway and Beadway, may forbid it even though it is described in their myths (Reichard, 1950, pp. 547–548). Other than Mountainway, the chant most often thought of as having a Dark Circle phase is Male Shootingway. Although Kluckhohn said that Female Shootingway possesses the Dark Circle phase (Kluckhohn and Wyman, 1940, p. 155), Mrs. Newcomb (field notes, 1939) doubted that the Female Mountain-Shootingway has been performed for many years.

Kluckhohn and Wyman (1938, pp. 5, 25) listed "Mountain Top Way, Male and Female Shooting Branches," as separate ceremonials and placed them in the Mountain Chant subgroup because their informants "without exception placed them with the Mountain Top Way ceremonials." Reichard, however, did not include them under these names in her "classification of ceremonies" (Reichard, 1950, chart 18, pp. 322–323). Apparently she relegated them to the branches of Male Shootingway as the Dark-circle-of-branches (Fire Dance, Corral Dance) branch, a feature that Kluckhohn and Wyman (1938, p. 11) also recognized as a phase of Holy Way ceremonials. Reichard's opinion is in essential agreement with Father Berard Haile's explanation that the name Mountain-Shootingway indicates only that when Shootingway presents a Fire or Corral Dance it borrows this feature from Mountainway (Haile, 1943, p. 44; 1947b, pp. 1–4). Father Berard, however, did not agree that a Shootingway performance with a Dark-circle-of-branches constituted a branch ceremonial of either Shootingway or Mountainway. He pointed out that the Corral Dance borrowed from Mountainway was merely an addition to the Shooting Chant. We may conclude, therefore, that Mountain-Shootingway, Shootingway Dark Circle of Branches, and Shootingway Corral or Fire Dance are all synonymous and that they are a phase of Shootingway rather than a branch. Father Berard (1947b, pp. 2–4) did say, however, that certain sandpaintings might be reserved for the Dark Circle phase of Shootingway, but that he was never successful in obtaining a basic legend for Mountain-Shootingway and that it is unlikely that one exists. Reichard (1950, p. 324) also stated that although details of procedure differ for different branches and phases of Male Shootingway, each emphasizing a different symbolic theme, there are no "differences of initial pattern or of myth, variations in interpretation being slight." She also said that some sandpaintings belonging to the Dark Circle phase can be recognized by a cross in the center, representing fire, but that in others there is no cross symbol to guide the observer.

In the files of the Museum of Navaho Ceremonial Art there is a description of a nine night Mountain-Shootingway ceremonial written by the late Mary C. Wheelwright that began on October 19 of an unspecified year. In that ceremonial two meal sprinklers (couriers) were painted, costumed, and dispatched on the fifth morning, as is done in a Mountainway ceremonial (see Matthews, 1887, pp. 424–427, fig. 52; Haile, 1946, pp. 1–10). Moreover, a Mountain-Shootingway chant, like Mountainway, may not be held until after the first snow or frost in the fall or after the first thunderstorm of the spring, and it is supposed to be held on some mountain (Newcomb, field notes). Nine-night Shootingway chants performed according to other phases are not subject to this seasonal restriction (see "Sun's House phase of Male Shootingway," above).

There are on record only 18 sandpaintings which were said by the recorders or collectors to be used in Mountain-Shootingway; however, ten other types of designs that also are used generally in Male Shootingway have been said (Newcomb and Reichard, 1937; Reichard, 1939) to be employed in the Dark Circle of branches (corral dance) phase (see Haile, 1947b, p. 3). These are Whirling Tail Feathers (No. 1, Walcott catalog); Slayer Twins in action (Slayer Twin quartet with Flint House and Mountains, Flint-armored Holy People, etc.; No. 2, Walcott catalog); Earth and Sky (may be used; No. 3, Walcott catalog); Cloud Houses (Nos. 5, 6, Walcott catalog); Sun, Moon, and Winds; Sky-reaching Rock, the double sandpainting (Reichard, 1939, p. 63; 1950, pp. 346, 704); Mixed Snake People and corn; Mixed Snake People (radial, see No. 13, Walcott catalog); Coiled (Endless) snakes; and Buffalo (radial, the home of the Buffalo People, see No. 15, Walcott catalog). Moreover, in the ceremonial described by Wheelwright the sandpainting of the Skies (No. 4, Walcott catalog) was the last one made, making eleven additional Shootingway designs used in this phase. The other three designs used in this ceremonial were of Snake People, Sky-reaching Rock (thus confirming Reichard), and buffalo. All of these have been discussed above. Only those sandpaintings in the first group (those specifically labeled Mountain-Shootingway sandpaintings) are discussed here. Nine types of design occur in this group: Slayer Twin quartet, People of the myth, dancers with various properties, Sky People (used exclusively in this phase), Thunders, swallowed by fish, Crooked Snake People, Sun or Moon clothed in snakes, and snakes on their house. The main theme symbols in these designs are described below.

Slayer Twin Quartet

Linear. Similar to the Slayer Twin quartet sandpainting used in Male and in Female Shootingway (see above).

People of the Myth

White Nostril People (sandpainting at Blue Water). Plate 39. Radial. Four pairs of male and female White Nostril People around central water, carrying plumes or feathered wands and tobacco pouches. These people are birdlike creatures (grebes, swans, monsters) with whom Cicada held an arrow-crossing contest and won by passing arrows through his body. References: Matthews, 1887, p. 437; Haile, 1947b, pp. 1–4; Wyman, 1965, pp. 85, 87. This painting was collected by Laura A. Armer at Black Mountain, Arizona, in 1929.

Mountain Sheep People at the Rock Rim. Plates 40, 41. Linear. Two quartets, one of male and the other of female Mountain Sheep People, on opposite sides of the center (the corral), carrying curved rainbows or feathered wands in one painting (Plate 40)

and decorated poles or poles and hoops in another (Plate 41), performing as dancers in the Dark Circle of Branches (corral). References: Matthews, 1887, p. 437; Haile, 1946, pp. 15, 34; 1947b, p. 2. These two paintings also were collected by Laura A. Armer at Black Mountain, Arizona, in 1929. Father Berard Haile (1947b, p. 2) remarked that the Mountain Sheep theme has a distinct Mountainway flavor, while the otter skin and bison headdresses and neckbands with attached whistle recall Shootingway.

Sky People

(Used exclusively in the Dark Circle phase of Male Shootingway)

Radial. Pairs of Sky People around the corral: Sky Man and Woman, Sun Man and Woman, Water Man and Woman, Summer Man and Woman. References: Newcomb and Reichard, 1937, pp. 59–60; Reichard, 1939, pp. 67–68, *pl. 22*; Wyman, 1960, p. 44.

Dancers

(with various properties)

Dancers with Sun, Moon, and Winds. See No. 19, Walcott catalog.
Dancers with Sun, Moon, and Wind wands. See No. 20, Walcott catalog.
Dancers with cactus. See No. 21, Walcott catalog.
Dancers with lightnings. See No. 22, Walcott catalog.

Thunders

Radial. The same as for Male Shootingway Holyway (see above).

Swallowed by Fish

Sandpainting at Slim Water. Plate 42. Radial. *Center:* black square with blue Big Fish and red flint knife. *Main theme symbols:* Horned Toad Man holding two flint knives at east, Holy Man carrying bow and arrow at west, Big Flies at south and north. *Quadrants:* Sun at southeast and northwest, Moon at southwest and northeast. *Paired guardians:* bats. As Father Berard Haile (1947b, pp. 2–3) has pointed out, "the theme of horned toad man being swallowed by 'big fish' whose sides he cuts with a flint knife and escapes" recalls the Swallowed by Fish episode of Male Shootingway, one of the two events depicted in the double sandpainting, Sky-reaching Rock (see No. 10, Walcott catalog).

Crooked Snake People

Radial. The same as for Male Shootingway Holyway; similar to a painting illustrated in Newcomb and Reichard (1937, *pl. 5*).

Sun or Moon Clothed in Snakes

Extended center. Pairs of crooked snakes crossed on the Sun or the Moon. Two paintings are the same as a Beautyway painting (see Wyman, 1957, *pl. 4*) and are similar to two Navaho Windway paintings (see Wyman, 1962, *figs. 33, 34*). There are two other paintings: in one, Monster Slayer is standing south of the Sun; in the other, Born-for-Water is standing south of the Moon, with Rainbow guardians and bear paired-guardians (Plate 43).

Snakes on Their House

Extended center. Crooked snakes crossed on circular black house. This sandpainting (No. 44, Huckel collection) is much like two Beautyway paintings shown in Wyman (1957, *fig. 3 (line)* and *pl. 3, color*) and is similar to snakes-on-house paintings of Male Shootingway Holyway (see Newcomb and Reichard, 1937, *pl. 2A*). References: Wyman, 1957, pp. 168, 188; 1960, p. 56.

SUMMARY OF SYMBOLISM

Of the 18 Mountain-Shootingway sandpaintings described above, seven are identical or similar to designs used in other ceremonials. The Slayer Twin quartet (WYUB), Thunders (BUYW), and Crooked Snake People (BUWY) are no different from such designs in Male Shootingway sandpaintings. The painting of Snakes on their house is like the same theme of Male Shootingway and even more like that of Beautyway, while the designs for Sun or Moon clothed in snakes (except for the two paintings which include the Slayer Twins) are also like Beautyway sandpaintings and are similar to some Navaho Windway designs. Swallowed by Fish depicts an event like that shown in the southern composition of the double sandpainting of Male Shootingway, but the design is entirely different.

Nine paintings uniquely characteristic of Mountain-Shootingway are those of People of the Myth (3), Sky People (1), and Dancers with various properties (5). As pointed out by Father Berard, these designs present a combination of Mountainway and Shootingway elements. Mountain Sheep themes, white faces (paint or mask; see Wyman, 1957, pp. 165–166), certain items of costume, and bears as paired guardians of the eastern opening are all characteristic of Mountainway. On the other hand, the pointed, red-feather headdresses, some with buffalo horns attached, Sun's House face stripes (Sky People), and other appurtenances remind us of Shootingway.

For such a small group of paintings there are many different directional color sequences: BUYW (7), BWUY (3), BUWY (2), WUYB (2), BYWP (1), BYUW (1), and WYUB (1). The centers (3 water, 4 corral, 1 house), headdresses, and guardians show about the same range of motifs as do those of Male Shootingway sandpaintings. The variety of paired guardians of the east is somewhat remarkable: Big Flies, bat and Sun's tobacco pouch, two bats, birds, bears, mountain lion and bear, crooked snakes, crooked lightnings, and stars. The White Nostril People and the Mountain Sheep People in the three paintings collected by Mrs. Armer at Black Mountain and the Sky People in paintings, by Miguelito (Red Point) show distinction of sex by shape of the head—round for males, square for females.

Since Mountain-Shootingway does not have a separate myth to be illustrated, it is a logical consequence that the majority of the sandpaintings used for this phase should illustrate the basic Male Shootingway legend and that the ones specifically assigned to it are either pictures of People of the Myth (with a few special features indicating the borrowing between Shootingway and Mountainway) or representations of dancers as they perform in the Dark Circle of Branches.

Male Shootingway Evilway Sandpaintings

Only 13 sandpaintings used in Male Shootingway ceremonials performed according to Evilway ritual have been recorded, and two of these are copies or versions of others. Moreover, in these 13 paintings there are only four (or seven, depending on viewpoint) different types of design represented—Slayer Twins within mountains, snakes, spiders, and baskets of arrows. The latter two are small sandpaintings for prayer or the sweat-emetic ceremony.

Slayer Twins Within Mountain

Extended center and radial. Black Monster Slayer (or hero of the myth, Holy Young Man), blue Born-for-Water, yellow Changing Grandchild, or pink (sparkling) Reared-in-the-earth (see Reichard, 1950, p. 55), surrounded by the four sacred mountains and protected by lightnings, sunbeam, or rainbow, in the cardinal positions. There may be wolf, mountain lion, eagle, and wildcat claws on the mountains. References: Kluckhohn and Wyman, 1940, p. 164; Wheelwright, 1949, p. 95; Wyman, 1962, pp. 78–79; 1967a, p. 6, *fig. 1 (halftone)*; cf. Kluckhohn and Wyman, 1940, *fig. 10 (line)*. A variation of this painting has the same design (with the hero or Monster Slayer) except that it has a black Endless Snake guardian coiled around the south, west, and north mountains. References: Newcomb, 1936, *p. 24 (halftone)*; 1940, *p. 14 (halftone)*; New Mexico Association on Indian Affairs, Indian Art Series No. 11 *(halftone)*; Haile, 1950, pp. 219–224, with a *color illustration (p. 224)*; Reichard, 1950, p. 715, *fig. 27 (line)*.

Snakes

Big Snakes. Radial. Four Big Snakes around a black big star. References: Wyman, 1957, pp. 167–168; 1962, pp. 297–298.
Crooked snakes. Radial. Four crooked snakes around a blue big star; black straight snake guardian. Linear (quartet); small prayer painting.
Coiled (Endless) snakes. Radial. The same as for Male Shootingway Holyway (see above).

Spiders

Radial. Five spiders (center and cardinal positions) each on a web. Small prayer painting. References: Wyman and Bailey, 1964, p. 148, *pl. 5H (line)*. The form of the figures is suspiciously realistic, so this may not be a reproduction of an actual sandpainting.

Baskets of Arrows

Radial. Four baskets, each containing four arrow points, around central fire; crooked and straight lightnings in quadrants; crooked lightning or rainbow garland guardian. Sweat-emetic small sandpainting. (See Plate 44.)

SUMMARY OF SYMBOLISM

Only two of the four design types among the paintings recorded for the Evilway ritual of Male Shootingway are uniquely characteristic of this ceremonial— Slayer Twins within Mountains, and Baskets of Arrows (a special drypainting for the sweat-emetic ceremony). A third one, the small prayer painting of spiders, possibly should be included, if it is valid. That would leave only one design, the Slayer Twins, as the characteristic large sandpainting of the Evilway ritual. The snake paintings are no different from those employed in other ceremonials. The painting of Big Snakes around black Big Star is identical to a Big Starway sandpainting except that the snakes are headed in the opposite direction; and the painting of crooked snakes around a blue star is similar to other Big Starway designs. Moreover, the bow and arrow paired guardians remind us of the bows and arrows commonly seen in Big Starway paintings of stars and snakes. Indeed, we might suspect syncretism or confusion of some sort on the part of the informant or the recorder, perhaps stemming from the fact that Big Starway is usually performed today according to Evilway ritual. The small prayer painting of crooked snakes in linear arrangement does not differ from a Male Shootingway Holyway design, and the painting of coiled (Endless) snakes is identical to this design in Holyway sandpaintings. Moreover, Reichard (1950, p. 715) tells of seeing the Sun, Moon, and Winds used separately as prayer paintings; and the sandpainting of the Red Snake People from Red Mountain (Reichard, 1939, pl. 16) is said to be used in Evilway ritual as well as for cases requiring protection from dangers—for example, lightning (Reichard, 1939, p. 56). Apparently, the Evilway ritual, for its own purposes, does not hesitate to draw upon certain sandpaintings also used in Holyway.

The directional color sequence of the snake and spider paintings is BUYW (from north to south in the linear composition of crooked snakes), the common danger sequence. That of the Slayer Twin paintings is WUYB, the other common sequence; this is puzzling, for here too we would expect a danger sequence.

The Mrs. Charles D. Walcott Collection

The Walcott collection of reproductions of Navaho sandpaintings is significant for several reasons. These paintings are among the earliest reproductions of sandpaintings that have been collected. Outside of the few recorded from Nightway and Mountainway by Stevenson and Matthews around the turn of the century, only three other major collections have reproductions that were made during the first two decades of the twentieth century. Some of the paintings in the Huckel collection were collected between 1902 and 1905; the Wetherill collection was made between 1910 and 1918; and a very few of the paintings in the Haile collection date from 1908. Also, the Walcott collection is one of the three (or possibly four) of the ten major collections that contain paintings made directly by native informants. The others are the Huckel, the Wetherill, and, possibly, the Haile collections. Records made by Navahos themselves are more valuable, of course, than those that have passed through the hands of non-Navaho recorders.

In the Walcott collection, which is in storage at the United States National Museum, are 28 painted reproductions (USNM Nos. 377450–76) of Navaho sandpaintings. The paintings are framed under glass—individually, except for two that are on the same piece of cloth (USNM 377457)—but they are available for study. Also, 8-by-10-inch photographs (BAE negatives 2457–b–1—27) of the individual paintings are in the files of the National Anthropological Archives, Smithsonian Institution.

The collection also includes four secular pictures (USNM Nos. 377477–80, BAE negatives 2457–b–28—31) of ceremonial scenes that show dancers or masked impersonators of the Ye'i performing in Nightway, or riders carrying the rattlestick in Enemyway.

The paintings are on dark tan-colored cloth, simulating the tan background of ordinary sand used in actual practice. The pigments used were native ones, mixed with some native adhesive agent, opaque commercial watercolors, and some commercial oils. The native pigments and commercial watercolors were applied with a sharpened stick, and the oils were applied with a brush. In a letter, Mrs. Montague (see below) wrote that "One can detect the cases where the worker experimented with a brush, and in one or two instances with oils, to return to his pointed stick." The colors vary somewhat, but in all cases they were intended to approximate the colors of the standard black, blue, yellow, white, pink, red, and brown dry pigments employed in making actual sandpaintings.

HISTORY OF THE COLLECTION

On 7 November 1932, Mrs. Eleanor Murphy Montague, who then was living in Carmel, California, wrote Mrs. Herbert Hoover that her father, Matthew M. Murphy, had suffered severe financial losses and was obliged to sell his collection of reproductions of Navaho sandpaintings, and that she thought Stanford University might be interested in purchasing it. Either this letter was forwarded to the Smithsonian Institution or Mrs. Montague wrote to the Institution on the same date, for on 21 November the Smithsonian advised her that it had a prospective purchaser and asked that she send the paintings on approval. On 1 December 1932, Dr. Charles G. Abbot, Secretary of the Smithsonian Institution, notified Mrs. Charles D. Walcott [8] (the prospective purchaser) that the paintings had arrived and that Mr. M. W. Stirling, then chief of the Bureau of American Ethnology, and Dr. Frank H. H. Roberts, Jr., had examined them

---

[8] The late Mary Vaux Walcott, widow of Charles Doolittle Walcott, Secretary of the Smithsonian Institution, 1907–1927. Charles Doolittle Walcott was one of the most eminent paleontologists of his time. He served as Secretary of the Smithsonian Institution for 20 years, from January 31, 1907, to the day of his death, February 9, 1927 (see Oehser, 1949, pp. 141–166). Previous to this he had been director of the United States Geological Survey for 13 years, and before that was an assistant geologist, so his span of service with the United States Government covered 48 years. Moreover, he had received an honorary appointment with the Smithsonian Institution in 1883 as curator of invertebrate fossils in the National Museum, so his connection with the Smithsonian actually lasted throughout 44 of those years.

and had found them much better than they had hoped. The purchase (for $2,000) was concluded on 5 December 1932. Mrs. Walcott donated the collection to the Bureau of American Ethnology, Smithsonian Institution, early in 1935, and on 12 February of that year a special viewing of the collection was held in the foyer of the Museum of Natural History. The collection was transferred to the United States National Museum on 21 March of the following year.

The 28 paintings in the collection had been made for Murphy, a trader and Navaho agent, by an old singer called Big Lefthanded.[9] In letters to Mrs. Montague, Dr. Abbot made several attempts to obtain information concerning the singer and the making of the paintings, but these queries were met with constant refusal to divulge anything at all about him. The excuse given was that Mr. Murphy had pledged himself not to make the name of the singer known, and that he wished to wait awhile before releasing any information since living relatives of the singer might resent it.[10] Mrs. Montague did say that her father's headquarters were at Tuba City during his term as agent,[11] so it seems that Big Lefthanded lived either near there or perhaps near Indian Wells, Arizona, since a note with one of his secular paintings now in the Museum of Northern Arizona reads "obtained by Murphy, trader and Indian agent at Indian Wells, Arizona, in the early 1900's" (see Wyman, 1967, pp. 2–3).

The documents with the paintings are similarly equivocal as to when the paintings were made.

In her letter to Mrs. Hoover, Mrs. Montague wrote:

When he went as Agent to the Navajo in 1905, they were in the seventh year of an extreme drought. It was broken soon after his arrival. He was given credit. Other circumstances helped to bring him into good repute, experiences with an old Medicine man too lengthy to relate here. The most compelling reason, however, is the old priest's grief over the old prophecy, that when the Sand Paintings should no longer be made, the Tribe should cease to be. . . . My father suggested him placing the paintings in their original condition, that is on buckskin, as Holy Young Man had received them, and in this way prevent the tribe perishing. Buckskin in such quantity or size was not available, so the work was done on cotton cloth; tapped on with a sharpened stick, for the man had never seen a brush. . . . The time occupied in this intermittent work was nearly seven years.

We may assume then, that the paintings were made between 1905 and 1912.

In her letter of 28 November 1932, Mrs. Montague wrote: "Beside the . . . Sand Paintings, there are four other [secular] pictures (not Sand Paintings) which my father will be happy to present to the acquirer of the paintings. . . . There is another picture in this group, which I will send later, the best of the lot from an artistic standpoint, I think: a man and a woman in costume performing a dance of the Mountain chant." The last-mentioned painting never reached the Smithsonian; it was purchased by the late Katherine Harvey who bequeathed it, along with other American Indian watercolors, to the Museum of Northern Arizona in 1963 (MNA 2363, C566). This painting and the four secular paintings in the Walcott collection are described and illustrated in an article by Wyman (1967, pp. 1–13, figs. 1–5).

FIELDWORK IN REGARD TO THE COLLECTION

No identifications, notes, or information of any kind concerning the paintings had been received with the collection from Mrs. Montague. Mr. Stirling and Dr. Roberts interviewed a delegation of Navaho Indians who visited Washington in 1935 shortly after the paintings had been received, but the results of this interview (BAE MS. No. 3924–A) were of little value in interpreting the paintings. In the summer of 1938 the Bureau of American Ethnology, through Mr. Stirling, employed Mrs. Franc J. Newcomb[12] of Albuquerque, New Mexico, to work with Navaho Indian informants on the reservation. Mrs. Newcomb,

---

[9] In notes and letters that accompanied the paintings, Big Lefthanded is referred to as Old Hostin Claw or as Klah-tso. "Claw" and "Klah" are attempts to write, in letters of the alphabet, the sound of the Navaho word that means "lefthanded." This Navaho word begins with a phoneme—the glottalized voiceless lateral affricate—that is very difficult for us to pronounce; and it is impossible for us to render its sound accurately by means of the alphabet. Perhaps this phoneme may best be transcribed as *tl'* (hence, *tl'ah*). "Tso" is a transcription of a Navaho word meaning "big."

[10] Hearing that Matthew Murphy's son Richard was living in Oak Run, California, the present author wrote to him in the summer of 1967 to obtain more information, but the letters were not answered.

[11] The head government man at Tuba City in the early days was not exactly an agent—his title was superintendent of the Western Navajo School—but he functioned as administrative officer for the entire western Navajo area. Matthew M. Murphy succeeded Milton J. Needham in that position at the beginning of December 1904 and served until November 22, 1907, when he was succeeded by Stephen Janus. By February 25, 1908, Murphy had been appointed special allotting agent, and he worked on allotting programs at Moenkopi and around the Hopi villages and adjoining tracts until March 1911. Shortly thereafter Murphy returned to his home in Carmel, California, and in 1916 he was living in Oak Run, California. There is no record as to whether Murphy ever returned to the reservation or whether he was ever on the reservation before he was appointed superintendent at Tuba City. (Information supplied by David M. Brugge, anthropologist for the Navajo Land Claim, Window Rock, Arizona.)

[12] Mrs. Newcomb, formerly an Indian trader's wife, had spent many years studying Navaho ceremonials in the vicinity of their trading post at Newcomb, New Mexico, and elsewhere, and had recorded in water color more sandpaintings than any other single person. All of one important collection (Bush collection) and the majority of another, the largest collection in existence (MNCA), are her work and her private collection in Albuquerque (Newcomb collection) contains several hundred reproductions. Moreover, she was the author or co-author of several papers and books on Navaho sandpaintings, mythology, and ceremonialism.

who had been supplied with photographs of the reproductions, obtained specific information relating to the paintings from seven informants, mostly during June and July of 1938. In May 1939 she sent Dr. Stirling the last batch of manuscript, which totaled about 155 typewritten pages. More than half of that manuscript, however, although containing interesting and important information, is not directly related to the collection, and much of the pertinent information corresponds with that already recorded and published by others. The names of Mrs. Newcomb's informants, along with other data concerning them, are listed below. The ages indicated for some of the informants are as approximated in 1938.

Judge Yellowhair, southwest of Indian Wells (west of Big Reed), Arizona; age, 68(?); singer of Mountain-Shootingway (pupil of Rock Canyon One and Curly Hair); headman of his district for two years, around 1920; Navaho judge from about 1923 to 1935.

Bitter Water (clan), near White Cone, Arizona; age, 55(?); singer of Shootingway and Female Mountainway; respected singer in his district.

Canyon People's Son (Plumeway Singer), White Cone, Arizona; singer of Female Plumeway.

Horse Herder, Chinle, Arizona; singer of Navaho Windway (pupil of Windway Singer).

Windway Singer, Sweetwater, Arizona; singer of Navaho Windway.

Slim White, home locality not stated; singer of Big Starway.

Large Man, White Cone, Arizona; singer of Nightway and Coyoteway.

CATALOG OF THE COLLECTION

Only seven (or possibly eight) of the twenty or so Navaho Chantways known to have used sandpaintings are represented in the Walcott collection, and five (or six) of these chantways are represented by only one painting (or two paintings) apiece. Most (18) of the paintings are from Male Shootingway; four are from Mountain-Shootingway; and two are from Beautyway, although one of the latter (No. 24 in the catalog) may be used in Mountainway or in both chants. Big Starway, Nightway, Plumeway, and Navaho Windway are represented by one painting each.

In the numerical listing which follows, the title of the sandpainting usually is a free English rendering of the Navaho name, but in cases where such a rendering would not be meaningful the Navaho name either is paraphrased or the painting is given a descriptive title.

The United States National Museum catalog number for the painting is followed (in parentheses) by the Bureau of American Ethnology (BAE) negative number of the pertinent photograph and then by the dimensions (given in inches) of the painting. The names and museum abbreviations under "Other collections" refer to those collections that contain a copy (when so indicated) of the particular reproduction or that have a painting identical or similar to it. If a similar painting is from a different chantway, the name of such chant follows in parentheses. "MNA file" refers to card numbers in the Wyman sandpainting file in the archives of the Museum of Northern Arizona; these numbers are preceded by the letters SC (Shootingway), MSC (Mountain Shootingway), BSC (Big Starway), BTC (Beautyway), NC (Night-

way), PC (Plumeway), or NWC (Navaho Windway). For example, "SC 13–17" refers to card numbers 13 through 17 filed under Shootingway in the archives. The citations under "References" indicate publications that contain text descriptions and illustrations (italicized) of similar sandpaintings or reproductions. A reference to a similar painting from a different chantway is followed by the name of the chant in parentheses.

The "Main theme category" of the painting corresponds to a category of the main theme symbols as listed in Table 3.

The information under "Description" is presented in the following order: composition (as *linear, radial,* or *extended center*), with the color sequences of the main theme symbols in the cardinal positions for a radial composition (east, south, west, north—the Navaho "sunwise" circuit) and positioned from south to north for a linear composition. Abbreviations for color are as follows: B, black; W, white; U, blue ("ultramarine," actually a bluish gray mixture of charcoal and white sand); Y, yellow; P, pink (sparkling; substituted for white in certain sandpaintings); R, red. Abbreviated descriptions then are given of the locality *Center* symbolizing the locality of the scene represented or symbolized; of the *Main theme symbols* (again in position sequence); of symbols in the *Quadrants* (southeast to northeast, "sunwise"); of the *Foundation bar* on which the main theme symbols stand; of the encircling *Guardian* of the painting ("Rainbow" indicates the Rainbow supernatural, or Goddess; "rainbow garland" or "mirage garland" indicates the nonanthropomorphized garland, or "rope," with feathered ends); and of the *Paired*

Guardians, which indicate the symbols at the eastern opening (south, north).

Subsequent paragraphs contain comments in regard to the subject's relationship to the myth, remarks made by Mrs. Newcomb's informants, interpretations of symbolism, and the like.

Male Shootingway

1. WHIRLING TAIL FEATHERS

Plate 1

USNM 377453 (BAE neg. 2457-b-4), 24⅞ by 26¼. [Other Collections: MNCA (copy); Huckel; Haile; Bush; Reichard. MNA file: SC 13–17. References: Newcomb and Reichard, 1937, pp. 34–36, 77, 87, *pl. 34 (color)*; Reichard, 1939, pp. 46–48, *fig. 4 (line)*; Wyman, 1960, p. 47.]

Alternative titles.—Holy People overcome Whirling-tail-feather; tail feather turned around; blue tail feather.

Main theme category.—*Holy People in action.*

Description.—*Radial;* BBWW (People), UBWY (Sun, Moon, and Winds), WUYR (feathers). *Center:* white Whirling Tail Feather (Moon), surrounded by WUYR feathers. *Main theme symbols:* Holy Man, Holy Boy, Holy Woman, Holy Girl, each holding a tail-feathered arrow and a bow which touches a Whirling Tail Feather (or basket containing a cosmic body). *Quadrants:* UBWY Whirling Tail Feathers (or blue Sun, Black Wind, white Moon, Yellow Wind, in feathered baskets). *Guardian:* rainbow garland (or mirage; the colors appear to be scumbled, making it difficult to identify). *Paired Guardians:* Sun, Moon.

This sandpainting illustrates at least two different mythic episodes. In the myth of Male Shootingway by Blue (Gray) Eyes of Lukachukai, Arizona (recorded by Father Berard Haile, see Newcomb and Reichard, 1937, pp. 34–36), Monster Slayer in the form of Holy Man visited a forbidden place where he found a dangerous wheel-like, whirling object called Whirling Tail Feather. He overcame it by means of his bows and arrows, and he was given the picture of the Holy People overcoming it by it by its keeper, Turtledove Man.

In the myth by Red Point (Miguelito) of Ganado, Arizona (recorded by Herman Schweizer, see Wyman, 1960, pp. 27–28), Holy Man and Holy Boy while visiting their father, the Sun, were tested by him in various ways. In order to ascertain the extent of their power he asked them to take down the sun. Returning to earth, they were joined by Holy Woman and Holy Girl, and the four, standing in the four directions, pulled down the Sun and Moon and the

Black and Yellow Winds with their bows. In the painting these cosmic bodies are shown resting in feathered baskets while the Holy People turn them around with their bows before taking them down (Reichard, 1939, pp. 46–48).

According to Judge Yellowhair, Mrs. Newcomb's informant, the Holy People are pushing the orbs around the center with their bows because these bodies have so much power that even the Holy People cannot handle them directly without being harmed. Thus, this sandpainting is a companion picture and preliminary to another called Taking Down the Sun (Reichard, 1939, p. 48, fig. 5; MNA file, SC–18), in which the Holy People, holding hide rattles and baskets to receive the orbs, pull down with their bows the Sun, Moon, and Winds, represented with horns as they usually are in sandpaintings (see Wyman, 1960, pp. 47–48).

In this sandpainting the Holy People have brown unmasked faces; the male figures have black bodies bearing longitudinal white zigzag lightnings; and females are white and wear many-colored dresses. All wear the pointed red feather headdress characteristic of Shootingway; yellow and brown feathered strings of otter skin dangle from wrists and elbows; and a decorated whistle, presumably attached to an otter skin collar, hangs by the right side. The figures stand on red and blue rainbow-bar foundations. The encircling guardian has bunches of five feathers at the quadrantal ends and corners. Usually these are white with black tips at the southeast, blue at the southwest, red with black tips at the northwest, and black at the northeast end, representing feathers of the eagle, hawk (or bluebird), red-shafted flicker, and magpie. According to Mrs. Newcomb these groups of feathers may represent the four sacred mountains of the cardinal directions (see Wyman, 1962, pp. 78, 79).

This sandpainting may be used in the Dark Circle of Branches (Corral Dance) phase of Male Shootingway; that is, in Mountain-Shootingway. Mrs. Newcomb's informant, Bitter Water, said that this painting is derived from the feathers that dance in the basket on the final night of a Mountain chant (see No. 19 below). The feathers were placed in baskets and taken to the Mountainway ceremonial. Judge Yellowhair said that many such pictures were omitted from ceremonial practice because they were too powerful.

2. SLAYER TWIN QUARTET WITH FLINT HOUSE AND MOUNTAINS

Plate 2

USNM 377452 (BAE neg. 2457-b-3); 28¾ by 26¾. [Other Collections: MNCA (copy); Huckel; Bush;

Reichard; Harvey. MNA FILE: SC 39–44. REFER-ENCES: Newcomb and Reichard, 1937, pp. 34, 48, 49, *pl. 17* (*color*); Reichard, 1939, pp. 64, 65, *pls. 18, 19* (*color*); 1950, p. 704, *fig. 23* (*line*); Wyman, 1960, pp. 42, 43.]

ALTERNATIVE TITLES.—Flint-armored Arrow People; Flint People.

MAIN THEME CATEGORY.—*Slayer Twins in action.*

DESCRIPTION.—*Radial; BYUP. Center:* black Flint Mountain (Spruce Hill, Gobernador Knob, New Mexico) with Changing Woman's house on it; Emergence Place with yellow-blue and black-white ladders, surrounded by the four sacred mountains with trees on them. *Main theme symbols:* Slayer Twin quartet, flint-armored; protected at feet, waist, and head by black-white crooked male lightning (Monster Slayer), yellow-white crooked sunbeams (changing Grandchild), red-blue straight female lightning (Born for Water), and red-blue rainbows (Reared-in-the-Mountain); carrying flint club, five lightnings, sunbeams or rainbows, and red Sun's tobacco pouch; and standing on rainbow-bars. *Quadrants:* blue corn, blue beans, black squash, black tobacco. *Guardian:* white-black crooked (male) lightning. *Paired guardians:* bat (Sun's tobacco pouch, which usually accompanies bat, is omitted).

This sandpainting refers to the struggle of the Sun, aided by his children—the Slayer Twins and their counterparts—to persuade Changing Woman to move to the new home made for her at the west by the Sun (see Newcomb and Reichard, 1937, pp. 34, 49). Its center is a combination of the centers of two paintings (Huckel, Nos. 10, 11, illustrated in Reichard, 1939, pls. 18, 19; see Wyman, 1960, pp. 42, 43) that are called The Four Mountains (spruce side by side) and Flint House (the house-of-many-points). According to Red Point (Miguelito), who made the two paintings, the black center represents Spruce Hill (Gobernador Knob, New Mexico) with the house of Changing Woman on it, and the surrounding mountains represent another phase of the home of the Slayer Twins or of their mother, "the place where spruce grew down the sides of the mountains."[13] In actual practice, the mountains are made in relief over heaps of sand, and sprigs of real spruce and fir are stuck into them. Bitter Water, one of Mrs. Newcomb's informants, said that the center is a tall black mountain with a hole in the top (volcanic cone) located somewhere in the northeast, and the only way to get down into this pit is on a ladder of sunlight or a shaft of black and white lightning. This place, known as Flint Mountain, is where the warriors

obtained flint to make their armor and weapons. The mountains are where the Flint People live. The northern warrior wears sparkling flint (pink in a sandpainting).

This sandpainting may be used in the Dark Circle of Branches (Corral Dance) phase of Male Shootingway; that is, in Mountain-Shootingway.

3. EARTH AND SKY

PLATE 3

USNM 377460 (BAE neg. 2457-b-11), 21¾ by 24⅛. [OTHER COLLECTIONS: Huckel; Wetherill (Blessingway); Haile; MNCA; Bush; Newcomb, Oakes (Earthway); ASM. MNA FILE: SC 47–52. REFER-ENCES: Coolidge and Coolidge, 1930, p. 230, *illustration on p. 222* (*halftone*); Sloan and LaFarge, 1931, *pl. 10* (*halftone*); Newcomb and Reichard, 1937, pp. 36, 55, *fig. 5* (*line*); Reichard, 1939, p. 45; Douglas and D'Harnoncourt, 1941, *p. 29* (*color*); Wyman, 1952, pp. 72–75, 80–81; 1960, pp. 43–44; Newcomb, Fishler, and Wheelwright, 1956, *fig. 22* (*line*); Quarterly, Southwestern Association on Indian Affairs, 1967, vol. 4, *p. 8* (*halftone*). Reproductions of the Earth or the Sky, as separate paintings, have been illustrated as follows: Wheelwright, 1949, *pp. 147, 149, 153, 155* (Blessingway, formerly attributed to Upward Reachingway or to Beautyway; *color*); 1956, *pl. 9* (Sky, Big Starway; *color*); Wyman, 1952, *figs. 32, 33* (Blessingway; *line*); O'Bryan, 1956, *fig. 3* (Earth; *line*); Newcomb, Fishler, and Wheelwright, 1956, *fig. 15* (Sky; *line*); Wyman and Newcomb, 1963, *fig. 3* (Earth, Big Starway; *halftone*); Illustrated London News, 1964, vol. 244, no. 6507 (18 April), supplement, *p. iv* (Earth; *color*).]

MAIN THEME CATEGORY.—*Cosmic and Celestial Beings.*

DESCRIPTION.—*Linear; UB. Main theme symbols:* blue Earth, black night Sky. *Guardian:* Rainbow. *Paired Guardians:* blue Sun, White Moon.

This sandpainting may be used in the Sun's House phase of Male Shootingway or in the Dark Circle of Branches (Corral Dance) phase (Mountain Shootingway). A reproduction similar to this one was the last of four paintings for the extinct Earthway that were collected by Maud Oakes in 1946; it now is in MNCA (Oakes collection). According to some informants, the sandpainting may be used on the last day of any ceremonial, although this is doubtful. Mrs. Newcomb said that she had always seen it used on the last day of Shootingway, "as it represents a consummation of perfection, power, and benefaction." Drypaintings of the Earth or of the Sky may be made separately for Blessingway, Big Starway, and Plumeway.

---

[13] All quotations (and references to statements) of informants included in the discussions of the paintings in the collection are from Mrs. Newcomb's field notes.

The blue Earth at the south, wearing "the turquoise dress of summer sky outlined with yellow pollen, and with hands and feet of pollen indicating fertility, sits on black mist held together by a rainbow" (Bitter Water). The black night Sky at the north also has pollen hands and feet; it is outlined with white morning light, and sits on a cloud of blue mist bound with a rainbow. Both figures wear the pointed red Shootingway headdress with attached eagle and turkey-tail feathers and a mask (or face paint) of Sun's House stripes—yellow on chin, blue, black, and white on forehead. Horns marked with lightnings are attached to the sides of their heads (imitations of buffalo horns are used in an actual Shootingway headdress) and a line of pollen (or white corn meal) connects their mouths. The patterns on their chests, arms, and legs—of white moon (Earth) or blue sun (Sky) with straight (female) or crooked (male) rain streaks and cloud symbols—are like the designs painted on a female or male patient in an actual ceremonial. Earth holds an ear of yellow corn and a white shell basket of yellow corn pollen. Sky holds the Sun's red tobacco pouch and an ear of corn. The black circle in the center of Earth represents the lake which filled Emergence Place after the people had emerged from the underworlds. From it grow yellow corn, blue beans, black squash (yellow flowers), and black tobacco—the four sacred plants brought from below. The Milky Way is depicted across Sky's chest, and various stars and constellations are on his body. Bitter Water remarked that "Mother Earth and Father Sky must be identical in shape and size, since they are the two halves of a whole creation laid side by side, like the two halves of an evenly cut melon."

4. THE SKIES

Plate 4

USNM 377455 (BAE neg. 2457-b-6), 28⅝ by 27⅝. [Other Collections: Huckel; Haile; ASM; MNCA; Bush (similar); Reichard; Harvey; Ganado; Stockholm. MNA File: SC 53-68. References: Newcomb and Reichard, 1937, pp. 58-59, *fig. 9 (line)*, see also *pl. 18 (color)*; Reichard, 1939, pp. 43-44, *fig. 2 (line)*; Leighton and Leighton, 1944, *p. 68 (halftone,* of actual sandpainting); Schevill, 1947, *frontispiece (color)*; Wyman, 1960, p. 45.]

ALTERNATIVE TITLES.—The four with tail-feathers; the Sun's painting.

MAIN THEME CATEGORY.—*Cosmic and Celestial Beings.*

DESCRIPTION.—*Radial;* WUYB. *Center:* blue Sun, Black Wind, white Moon, Yellow Wind. *Main theme symbols:* trapezoidal skies; White Dawn, Blue Day, Yellow Twilight (Evening Light; Sunset); Black Night

(Darkness). *Quadrants:* blue corn, blue beans, black squash, black tobacco. *Guardian:* rainbow connecting Day, Evening, and Night Skies. *Paired Guardians:* black bat (Sun's tobacco pouch omitted).

This sandpainting, given by the Sun to his children (Slayer Twins; Holy Man and Boy), represents the passing of the Sun through the hours of the day. According to Judge Yellowhair it is a picture of the four beings who emerged from the underworld to drain the new earth, which was still covered with water. After giving their calls in the four directions they went to the edges of the world, where they may still be found. In the painting they are given the earth-cloud form and twelve tail feathers, and also messengers (birds) for communication between them and earth people. The four plants represent the earth; the Sun, Moon, and Winds represent the sky; and above all these are the big tail-feathered ones.

Crooked (male) and straight (female) lines of rain extend from the Sun, Moon, and Winds to protective rainbow bars. The winds have whirlwinds (white cotton cords) on their heads, and all have eagle plumes. Sun and Moon also have turkey-tail feathers. A yellow bird ("pollen bird") perches on the corn tassels. On the eastern Dawn Sky with its black-tipped white feathers (rays of early morning light) are a yellow-headed blackbird, a blue mountain sheep, and a blue bird with white spots. On the southern Blue Sky are two yellow birds (wild canaries). On the western Evening Sky are two bluebirds, one with a black tail (blue swallow?). The northern Night Sky bears the usual Milky Way (crossed line), stars, and constellations (see Haile, 1947, p. 15).

A sandpainting of the Skies was the last one to be made in a Mountain-Shootingway performance witnessed by Mary C. Wheelwright.

5. CLOUD HOUSES

Plate 5

USNM 377472 (BAE neg. 2475-b-23), 38¾ by 36¾. [Other Collections: Bush. MNA File: SC 69-71. References: Newcomb and Reichard, 1937, p. 60, *pl. 20 (color)*.]

ALTERNATIVE TITLE.—Big house sandpainting.

MAIN THEME CATEGORY.—*Cosmic and Celestial Beings.*

DESCRIPTION.—*Radial;* UBWY. *Center:* blue Sun, Black Wind, white Moon, Yellow Wind. *Main theme symbols:* UBWY cloud houses, each bearing two cloud symbols and surmounted by two ears of corn; two cloud columns guarded by two feathers each; and a Sun, Moon, or Wind; all are of the same color as the house except for the guardian feathers on the blue and yellow houses, which are of contrast colors. *Guardian:* rainbow connecting south, west, and north houses.

The Sun, Moon, and Winds in the center and above the houses are the same as in Number 4. Since this painting is incomplete, the description of its details is reserved for Number 6, which is a complete version of the same fundamental design. Judge Yellowhair refused to discuss this painting, saying that it is an evil picture because it was not made right. The ears of corn lack feathers on either side for support; the cloud columns have no birds on them; and the Sun, Moon, and Winds above the houses face in the wrong direction, away from the houses.

6. CLOUD HOUSES

PLATE 6

USNM 377475 (BAE neg. 2457–b–26), 33½ by 35¼. [OTHER COLLECTIONS: Bush. MNA FILE: SC 69–71. REFERENCE: Newcomb and Reichard, 1937, p. 60, *pl. 20 (color)*.]

ALTERNATIVE TITLE.—Big house sandpainting.

MAIN THEME CATEGORY.—*Cosmic and Celestial Beings.*

DESCRIPTION.—*Radial*; UBWY. *Center:* blue Sun, Black Wind (male), white Moon, Yellow Wind (female). *Main theme symbols:* UBWY cloud houses (the eastern house is painted black, but since the cloud symbols on it are yellow and the cloud columns on it are blue, it must be the blue house). *Quadrants:* bunches of five red, black, white (black tips), and red (black tips) feathers. *Guardian:* Rainbow.

Each house bears two cloud symbols of contrast colors (black and white, and blue and yellow are called contrast colors). Surmounting each house are two ears of corn, two four-tiered cloud columns, and a Sun, Moon, or Wind, all of the same color as the house. Each ear of corn is guarded by four white feathers, two on a side. Above each cloud column is a bird—a blue bird with white spots and a yellow-headed blackbird at the east, two yellow birds with variegated spots at the south, two blue birds (one with a black tail) at the west, a yellow bird with a red tail and a yellow-red bird with a yellow tail at the north. The black streaks in the background represents the lines of powdered charcoal called "thin clouds" or "summer clouds," which are said to bring rain. These are put on a sandpainting after it has been completed. Judge Yellowhair said that the cloud symbols on the houses are windows or openings through which the Sun, Moon, and Winds can see the earth below. He said we see this in the morning or early evening when long rays of light or bars of shadow creep across the land, and that these houses are in the sky just above the horizon. That is why the clouds and the birds appear to be above them.

Like number 5, this sandpainting may be used in the Dark Circle of Branches (Corral Dance) phase of Male Shootingway; that is, in Mountain-Shootingway.

7. SUN'S HOUSE

PLATE 7

USNM 377462 (BAE neg. 2457–b–13), 21¾ by 16⅝. [OTHER COLLECTIONS: Huckel; Haile; MNCA; Bush; ASM; Ganado. MNA FILE: SC 85–94. REFERENCES: Reichard, 1934, *pp. 28 (illustration)*, 180–189; 1936, p. 110, *pl. 9b (halftone, of sandpainting blanket woven by Atlnaba, Red Point's daughter, from one of his paintings)*; 1939, pp. 42–43, *fig. 1 (line)*; Newcomb and Reichard, 1937, pp. 59–60, *pl. 19 (color)*; Schevill, 1945, cover *(halftone, of actual screen)*, pp. 3–5; 1947, *p. 120 (color)*; Wyman, 1960, pp. 46–47.]

ALTERNATIVE TITLE.—Big house sandpainting.

MAIN THEME CATEGORY.—*Cosmic and Celestial Beings.*

DESCRIPTION.—*Extended center and linear.* UWBY (Sun, Moon, Winds); BWUY (cloud columns). *Center:* YUBW (upwards) Sun's House; two sets of blue Sun, white Moon, Black Wind, Yellow Wind—one set in windows framed with rainbow in yellow bar at bottom and another on top of house—surmounted by two ears of white corn, each guarded by two white feathers; and BWUY four-tiered cloud columns, each with a bird over it (bluebird, blue bird with black tail, yellow bird with variegated spots, yellowheaded blackbird). *Guardians:* rainbow garland around entire house; black straight lightning(?) with white tips at east, rainbow-bar at south, white-black crooked lightning at west, white-yellow crooked lightning (light?) at north.

This sandpainting, given to Holy Man by the Sun, is a picture of the screen made of rods of wood (or reeds), which is a permanent property of the singer's bundle used in the Sun's House phase (chant with house) of Male Shootingway. It may be made when the singer does not own an actual screen. The sequence of colors on the Sun's House are the origin of the Sun's House stripes in the face painting of Shootingway (see Nos. 3, 17). Judge Yellowhair said that this painting is fundamentally the same as the Cloud House paintings (Nos. 5, 6) except that the four colored houses are placed one above the other and the windows are all in the lower one, while the ears of corn, cloud columns with birds, and Sun, Moon, and Winds surmount the whole. McAllester's informant, RC of Lukachukai, Arizona, told him that the Sun's House is made up of four houses, those of Yellow Wind, Sun, Dark Wind, and Moon (see the section on Sun's House phase of Male Shootingway).

8. FISH PEOPLE

FRONTISPIECE

USNM 377474 (BAE neg. 2457–b–25), 33½ by 35¼. [OTHER COLLECTIONS: MNCA (copy). MNA FILE: SC 106. REFERENCES: Newcomb and Reichard, 1937, p. 64; Wheelwright, 1946, p. 15; see No. 10, below, for references to the mythic motif, *Swallowed by Fish*.]

ALTERNATIVE TITLE.—Big Fish.

MAIN THEME CATEGORY.—*Water Creatures*.

DESCRIPTION.—*Radial; BUWY. Center:* black lake. *Main themes symbols:* BUWY Fish People holding an ear of corn and a basket of pollen. *Quadrants:* blue corn, blue beans, black squash, black tobacco. *Foundation bar:* rainbow bars. *Guardian:* Rainbow. *Paired Guardians:* black (or dark brown) beaver, otter.

This painting is unique in that it is the only one which has been recorded showing the anthropomorphized Fish People. Fish in their natural forms appear in the episode of Swallowed by Fish shown in the reproduction of the double sandpainting of Male Shootingway (Nos. 10, 11), in a single painting illustrating this episode in Mountain-Shootingway (Plate 43), and in several reproductions of sandpaintings of Plumeway. In one of the latter (MNCA, No. 4–12) four naturalistic Big Fish appear as main themes (although placed in the quadrants).

Canyon People's Son, one of Mrs. Newcomb's informants, assigned this painting to Plumeway, and it is interesting that he was the artist of the painting of naturalistic Big Fish mentioned above. It seems more likely, however, that the sandpainting belongs to Shootingway, as the Fish People wear the red Shootingway headdress (see No. 1). Swallowed by Fish does appear in one version of a Plumeway myth, also told by Canyon People's Son (Wheelwight, 1946, p. 15), but that story is decidedly different from all other recorded Plumeway myths, apparently being made up of motifs from the Origin Myth and Shootingway, with brief Plumeway episodes appended to it, so, it is likely that the author took the Fish motif from Shootingway. As a matter of interest, Canyon People's Son's account of the event as told to Mrs. Newcomb when he saw this sandpainting is given here:

One time when the Deer-Farmer was walking along the edge of the lake [shown in the center of the sandpainting] he saw a plant growing out of the water. It had leaves like wide reeds, and there were two ears of corn showing above the water, but many more under that. So when the snake or fish sandpaintings are made it is all right to put from twelve to twenty-four ears of corn on one stalk, because they are the People of the underworld where it grew that way. But in other sandpaintings, there are only two ears shown on each stalk, those being the ones that came above the water [see Wyman and Newcomb, 1962, pp. 47–50, fig. 6, for a discussion of twelve-eared corn and an illustration]. The Deer-

Farmer wanted to get this corn to plant in his fields, so he threw out a magic rainbow bridge across the lake and started to walk over to where he could pick the corn. But the Fish People caused his bridge to sag and disappear in the water near the middle of the lake, so that he went down into the water, was swallowed by a Big Fish, and was taken to the land of the Fish People. A long prayer goes with this Painting. The four plants that grow around the lake first grew in the land of the Fish People and were not known on this earth until the Deer-Farmer brought them back from there. The Fish People were the first to know the planting and harvesting rites.

9. HOLY MAN CAPTURED BY THUNDERS

PLATE 8

USNM 377465 (BAE neg. 2457–b–16), 23⅛ by 31¾. [OTHER COLLECTIONS: Huckel; MNCA; Reichard; ASM. MNA FILE: SC 109–112. REFERENCES: Newcomb and Reichard, 1937, p. 39; Reichard, 1939, pp. 57–58, 62, *fig. 6 (line)*; Shevill, 1947, *p. 30 (color)*; Wyman, 1960, p. 49.]

MAIN THEME CATEGORY.—*Thunders*.

DESCRIPTION.—*Radial; BYUP. Center:* black Holy Man carrying bow and arrow by the black lake, "on top of the. mountain where the Thunders live; the [BYUP] spikes around it are the high peaks of rock on which the Tunders perch" (Judge Yellowhair). *Main theme symbols:* BYUP Thunders. *Northeast Quadrant:* blue mountain sheep. *Guardian:* white-black crooked lightning. *Paired guardians:* bat (Sun's tobacco pouch omitted). "Thin clouds" of all colors in background (see No. 6).

Holy Man, his body bearing white zigzag lightning, stands east of the black lake near the home of the Thunders. According to Judge Yellowhair:

The points around it are arrow points, patterns for those given to earth people. The [BYUP] dragonflies around the lake fly ahead of a storm and warn people that the thunder is coming. The Thunders carry rain in their tails. When the tails are widespread rain falls; when they are narrow there is no rain. The curved lines by their tails are the reverberation of thunder.

Holy Man is attached to all the Thunders by white-black crooked lightning, yellow-white sunbeam, and red-blue female lightning and rainbow, indicating their capture of him and the means they used to take him up to their home in the sky for instruction. Above the head of each Thunder is an arrow point and a lightning, sunbeam, or rainbow. There are barbed (male) points and crooked (male) lightning and sunbeam at east and south, smooth (female) points and straight (female) lightning and rainbow at west and north. Holy Man was captured while hunting the mountain sheep, which was placed on Black Mountain (Jemez Mountains) by the Thunders to lure him.

This painting is combined with the painting of Swallowed by Fish to make the double sandpainting called Sky-reaching Rock, in which it is the northern composition (Nos. 10, 11). It seems to be the only one of the two paintings that is used by itself, although there is a reproduction (in MNCA) alleged to be of a Plumeway sandpainting made by Smiling Singer of Dilkon, Arizona, that depicts Swallowed by Fish. That painting, however, appears to be in every detail a copy of the southern composition of Number 10.

10. SKY-REACHING ROCK

PLATE 9

USNM 377473 (BAE neg. 2457–b–24), 36¾ by 47⅛. [OTHER COLLECTIONS: MNCA (including copy of part; see No. 9); Huckel; Wetherill; Haile; Bush; ASM; Stockholm. MNA FILE: SC 113–121. REFERENCES: Reichard, 1934, pp. 194–203, *illustration* (*color*) *on p. 194;* 1939, pp. 61–63; 1950, pp. 221, 704, 711; Newcomb and Reichard, 1937, p. 39, *fig. 3* (*line*); Wheelwright, 1946, p. 15 (Plumeway); 1958, pp. 21–22; Wyman, 1952, pp. 36–37; 1960, pp. 49–50; Mills, 1959, *frontispiece* (*color;* reversed).]

ALTERNATIVE TITLE.—The double sandpainting, Opposite-each-other.

MAIN THEME CATEGORY.—*Thunders and Water Creatures.*

DESCRIPTION.—Two *radial* compositions on each side of an *extended center;* WUYB (center and south), BYUP (north). *Extended center:* at west, Sky-reaching Rock, black with yellow top (pollen; in practice a tall cone of clay; see Plate 10) with four black lakes (bowls of water) around it, each with a duck on it (WUYB); white wolf and black bear east of the rock, and Black Thunder east of them (creatures who searched for Holy Boy in vain); at east center, blue Sun with four red feathers.

Southern composition (*Swallowed by Fish*).—*Center:* yellow Holy Boy carrying three flints (UBW), with which he cut his way out of the fish, and five blue medicine herbs, with which he healed the fish. *Main theme symbols:* WUYB Big Fish; a rainbow from the mouth of the eastern Fish surrounds Holy Boy's head and shoulders, indicating the swallowing. *South:* a blue, twelve-eared cornstalk rooted in a black pool with its tassels touching a blue mountain (Mount Taylor) with a black pool on it, where Holy Boy was captured. In practice, the mountain is made in relief, with a bowl of water sunk in it.

Northern composition (*Holy Man Captured by Thunders*).—*Center;* black Holy Man. *Main theme symbols:* BYUP Thunders. *East:* Black Mountain, where Holy Man was captured, with a blue mountain sheep on it, placed there by the Thunders to lure him. In practice, the mountain is made in relief with

a cup of water sunk in it to represent a lake, and the two trees growing on it are represented by real fir and spruce twigs stuck into it. This composition is the same as that of Number 9, except there is no lake in the center. This painting shows Holy Man leaving the earth, while Number 9 illustrates his arrival at the home of the Thunders.

Guardian: southern half, Rainbow, with head at southeast (sic!); northern half, white-black crooked lightning. *Paired guardians:* black beaver and otter.

The double sandpainting, the most elaborate of all sandpainting designs, illustrates the following episodes in the myth of Male Shootingway (see Spencer, 1957, pp. 120–121). The Thunders, some of which lived on top of Sky-reaching Rock, placed a mountain sheep on Black Mountain (Jemez Mountains; Hesperus Peak in Bitter Water's story) to lure Holy Man, who was out hunting. After Holy Man shot the sheep the Thunders took him to their sky home where they instructed him in ceremonial procedure. In the meantime, Holy Boy, who was hunting on Mount Taylor, tried to reach a twelve-eared cornstalk which had been placed in the middle of a pool to entice him. While trying to reach the cornstalk he fell into the water and was swallowed by a big fish and carried to the home of the Water People at the bottom of the lake. There he cut his way out of the fish by means of flint points, and he then healed the creature with medicine herbs (in other versions Holy Man cuts the fish and pulls his brother out). In Bitter Water's story, Holy Boy swam out to the cornstalk, and the big fish swam around him, creating a whirlpool which sucked him down under the lake. Then he was instructed in ceremonial lore by the Water People. By this time Holy Man had been returned to earth and, missing his younger brother, he enlisted the aid of ducks, Wolf, Bear, and a Thunder, but they searched in vain. Coming to the lake, Holy Man decided (or was told by Big Fly) that his brother was in the water, and he threw in offerings of jewels for his return. In Bitter Water's tale both Holy Man and Holy Boy are rescued by Talking God, Black God, and Water Sprinkler. Details of their return also vary in other versions of the myth. Finally ceremonials were held over the brothers. The ceremonials vary in nature and purpose in different versions of the myth. According to Bitter Water, the Fish People sang over Holy Boy in order to impart to him the ceremonial concerned with the planting, care, and fertility of seeds, especially corn, while the Thunders performed for Holy Man in order to give him their ceremonial for bringing rain. Then each brother performed his ceremonial over the other one, so that each learned the other's chant, and that is why both of their stories are now depicted in the same sandpainting.

Reproductions of ten versions of this sandpainting, including Numbers 10 and 11, are in various collections (see Table 5). Numbers 10 and 11, of course, were made by the same person; two other reproductions (one in the Huckel collection and one in the Stockholm collection) were made by Red Point (Miguelito), of Ganado, Arizona; and two others (one in the Wetherill collection and one in ASM) are slightly different copies of the same original (see discussion on versions of the double sandpainting, below). The other reproductions are by different singers. One of these (MNCA 8A–4A, the work of Blue Eyes' nephew from Newcomb, New Mexico) was made in colored sands and stabilized as a center piece for the main exhibition room of the Museum of Navaho Ceremonial Art.

Number 10 has several unique features as compared with the nine other versions (including No. 11). The Thunder who joined in the search for Holy Boy is black instead of yellow (in one version of the myth Yellow Thunder was said to live on top of Sky-reaching Rock). The presence of the Sun at east-center is difficult to explain. Perhaps it is there to remind us that Holy Man and Holy Boy are cognates of the Slayer Twins, sons of the Sun, or that the sandpainting was given to them by the Thunder People at the behest of the Sun. Holy Boy is yellow instead of black, and yellow is his proper color (Reichard, 1950, p. 238). The Big Fish have long curled tails instead of short forked ones. This is one of the features which indicate that the alleged Plumeway sandpainting mentioned under Number 9 (above) is a copy of a portion of Number 10. The cornstalk used to decoy Holy Boy is at the south of the painting in Number 10, whereas it is in the center in Number 11. The cornstalk extends from Sky-reaching Rock so as to lie beside Holy Boy, between him and the northern Big Fish, in the versions by Miguelito (Plate 12), and RC (Plate 13) and in the one in the Bush collection (see Table 5), while it lies north of the Fish in the versions

by Sam Chief (Plate 15), Gray Man (Plate 16), and Blue Eyes' nephew (Plate 14) and in the sandpainting photographed by Katherine Harvey (Plate 10). A bird perches on the corn tassels in only two versions. Having the head of the Rainbow guardian at the southeast is a feature unique not only for this painting but for all sandpaintings.

Numbers 10 and 11 share some unique features as compared with the other eight versions. In these two paintings there are four ducks instead of sixteen. In the other paintings the ducks are arranged in quartets of the four colors, stand on rainbow bars around Sky-reaching Rock, and carry male or female lightning, sunbeam, and rainbow in their beaks. There are no plants rooted in the pools around the rock, unless the colored rays springing from the pool at the bottom of the central cornstalk in Number 11 are meant to represent them. The cornstalk is twelve-eared; in the other versions it is the ordinary two-eared variety (see Wyman and Newcomb, 1962, p. 48). Moreover, it stands rooted in its own pool instead of growing from one of the pools around Sky-reaching Rock along with the beans, squash, and tobacco. The corn tassels are in contact with a blue mountain (Mount Taylor), while this mountain stands apart in the other versions—east or northeast of the southern composition—and has four colored quadrants, WUYB in four versions and BUWY and BUYW in two others. The corn is blue in all but one version (black, Haile collection). The black or brown otter and black Big Fly guarding Holy Man in south and north in all the other versions are missing. Features unique for No. 11 are given below.

This sandpainting is most commonly used for the Sun's House (chant with house) phase of Male Shootingway, but Reichard and Wheelwright saw it used in different performances of the Dark Circle of Branches (Corral Dance) phase (Mountain-Shootingway; Reichard, 1939, p. 63; 1950, p. 704). Reichard also saw it used in a Sun's House phase performed

TABLE 5.—*Known reproductions of the double sandpainting, Sky-reaching Rock*

Navaho artist	Locality	Date collected	Collector	Collection, item No.	Illustration in this paper
Big Lefthanded	Tuba City, Ariz.	1905–1912	Matthew M. Murphy	Walcott, Nos. 10, 11	Plates 9, 11
Yellow Singer (Sam Chief)	Oljeto, Utah	1910–1918	Louisa W. Wetherill	Wetherill, No. 11; and ASM, No. L–42	Plate 15
Red Point (Miguelito)	Near Ganado, Ariz.	1924	Herman Schweizer	Huckel, No. 28	—
Red Point	Near Ganado, Ariz.	1929–1930	Nils Hogner	Stockholm	Plate 12
Blue Eyes' nephew	Newcomb, N. Mex.	Before 1930	Franc J. Newcomb	MNCA, No. 8A–4A	Plate 14
Unknown	?	?	Franc J. Newcomb	Bush	—
Gray Man	Chinle Wash, Ariz.	1934	Father Berard Haile	Haile, No. 13	Plate 16
RC	Lukachukai, Ariz.	1957	David P. McAllester	MNCA, No. 8B–6	Plate 13

according to Injuryway (Red Inside) subritual (Reichard, 1950, p. 711).

11. SKY-REACHING ROCK

PLATE 11

USNM 377476 (BAE neg. 2457–b–27), 35⅞ by 46¾. [For similar reproductions in other collections and for references see No. 10.]

ALTERNATIVE TITLE.—The double sandpainting.

MAIN THEME CATEGORY.—*Thunders and Water Creatures.*

DESCRIPTION.—Two *radial* compositions on each side of center. WUYP (ducks), WYUB (south), BYUP (center, north, Water Monsters). *Center:* blue, twelve-eared cornstalk rooted in a black pool with BYUP rays (plants?) and its tassels touching a blue mountain (Mount Taylor) having a black lake on it. *Northwest:* yellow (pollen) Sky-reaching Rock, around which are four black lakes, with a duck on each (WUYP); yellow wolf and black bear east of the rock.

Southern composition (*Swallowed by Fish*).—*Center:* black Holy Boy carrying bow and arrow. *Main theme symbols:* WYUB Big Fish; the rainbow in the mouth of the eastern Fish touches Holy Boy's head.

Northern composition (*Holy Man Captured by Thunders*).—*Center:* black Holy Man carrying bow and arrow. *Main theme symbols:* BYUP Thunders. *Northeast:* Black Mountain, with two blue trees on it and a blue mountain sheep below it.

East, south, west, north: BYUP Water Monsters (in more or less cardinal positions around the entire design), who were among the Water People who instructed Holy Boy.

Guardian: white-black crooked lightning. *Paired guardians:* bat (Sun's tobacco pouch omitted).

Unique features that this painting shares with Number 10 have been discussed under the latter. Its unique features as compared with the nine other versions (including No. 10) are as follows. The corn decoy is in the center. The ducks are in the pools instead of above or around them. The wolf is yellow instead of white. There is no Thunder separate from the northern composition. The color sequence of the Big Fish is WYUB, a cross-arrangement (see Reichard, 1950, p. 223). The white Big Fish is in the east in Numbers 10 and 11 and also in a painting (in Stockholm collection) by Red Point (see Plate 12), but in all the other reproductions of the double sandpainting, including Red Point's other one (Huckel collection, No. 28, illustrated as frontispiece in Mills, 1959), the eastern Fish is black. Reichard (1950, p. 221) thought that this might correlate with the sex of the patient—black for a male, white for a female. The

color sequence of the Thunders is BYUP in all known versions of Holy Man Captured by Thunders, both in the double sandpainting or when used separately (see Reichard, 1950, p. 224). Holy Man and Holy Boy carry bows and arrows, but in the other versions Holy Man is not carrying anything and Holy Boy carries flints and medicine herbs. In Number 9, Holy Man also carries a bow and arrows. In these instances, apparently, Big Lefthanded did not choose to portray the dictum set forth in Bitter Water's myth: that, because Holy Man, becoming tired, had laid aside his bow and arrows he could be captured by the Thunders, who could not touch him as long as he was carrying them. The mountain sheep decoy is below Black Mountain instead of above or upon it. Other unique features are the Water Monsters, the crooked lightning guardian around the whole painting, and the bat guardian of the eastern opening.

VERSIONS OF THE DOUBLE SANDPAINTING

Since there are ten recorded versions of Sky-reaching Rock, well spaced in time and provenience, it is of interest to compare them further with respect to variations. (The ten versions are listed in Table 5.)

Many variations of the double sandpainting have been described above in discussing the unique features of Numbers 10 and 11. Aside from the minor variations commonly present among sandpaintings produced or reproduced by different singers—differences in size, proportions, and exact placing of various symbols, the shape and placing of the mountains, and the like—the most variable feature seems to be the encircling guardian. In four of the ten versions (Huckel; Stockholm; MNCA, by RC; Bush) and in a painting described by Reichard (Sun's House phase, Injuryway subritual) the guardian of the whole is the Rainbow, as in Plates 12 and 13 (see also, Reichard, 1934, p. 194; Newcomb and Reichard, 1937, fig. 3). In each case, Holy Man Captured by Thunders has a separate guardian of white-black or black-white crooked lightning. This design seems to require a lightning guardian, for in the other versions to be described it is surrounded by lightnings or the lightning portion of the guardian, and in all recorded versions of this design as a separate sandpainting the guardian is white-black crooked lightning. In two of the ten versions—Number 10 and one by Blue Eyes' nephew that is in MNCA (see Plate 14)—and in a painting described by Reichard (Mountain-Shootingway) the guardian has different halves; the southern half is a Rainbow (Number 10) or a feathered rainbow garland, and the northern half is white-black or black-white crooked lightning.

In two other versions—one in the Wetherill collection (see Plate 15) and one in the Haile collection (see Plate 16) and in a painting described by Reichard' (Mountain-Shootingway) each of the two compositions has its own separate guardian, a Rainbow (Wetherill collection) or rainbow garland around Swallowed by Fish, and the usual lightning guardian around Holy Man Captured by Thunders. In the painting in the Wetherill collection the two guardians do not encircle their compositions completely. The Rainbow partly encircles the Sky-reaching Rock complex, ending with its head just east of it, while the lightning guardian of the northern composition also terminates in the same place beside the Rainbow's head (see Plate 15). In the other copy of this painting (in ASM) both guardians (Rainbow's head and lightning arrow points) terminate in the center of the western side of the composition just opposite the Sky-reaching Rock complex. Both copies were made by Clyde A. Colville of Kayenta, Arizona, presumably from an original (now lost) by Sam Chief. In the double sandpainting of the Sun's House phase made by SM of Lukachukai, Arizona, and witnessed by McAllester in 1958 the guardians were remarkable—in fact, unique—in that there were two complete Rainbow supernaturals. Each composition had its own separate guardian as described above, while the entire sandpainting was surrounded by another Rainbow. In only one version (Number 11) is the entire guardian of crooked lightning.

The paired guardians of the eastern opening are quite uniform. Only five of the paintings have them, and in four of these they are beaver and otter. In one version (Number 11) the eastern guardian is a single bat.

Other variations, most of them probably insignificant, could be noted: the bear is south of the wolf in five paintings, and in two of these, both by Red Point, the feet of these animals are toward the east; the separate Thunder is missing in two (Number 11, and the one in the Wetherill collection) and is between wolf and bear and the Sky-reaching Rock in two (Haile; MNCA, by RC); the color sequence of the ducks is BUYW in four, WUYB in four, and WUYP in one (see Reichard, 1950, p. 221); in the seven paintings that have the four sacred plants the color sequence of the plants is UUBU in four, UUBB in two, and BUBU(?) in one; the Big Fish have legs as well as fins in five paintings; Holy Boy has five flints suspended around his neck (in addition to the flint he holds in his hand) in six paintings, one flint suspended from his neck in one painting (Plate 15), and additional medicine herbs in three paintings.

From the above description of unique features and variations it might seem that there has been consider-able change in Navaho sandpainting art during the last 60 years. Actually, however, bearing in mind the complexity of this particular design, there is little more variation in these versions of the double sandpainting than we find at any one time among the works by different singers. In fact, Big Lefthanded's two versions of this one sandpainting differ from each other almost as much as they do from those of later singers. All of the fundamental symbols and events are portrayed, and the existing variations mostly are of the same kind that have been common in sandpainting art throughout the years from which we have records. Perhaps the most strikingly unique feature of Big Lefthanded's two paintings is the twelve-eared cornstalk instead of the common two-eared variety, but in this the singer was adhering closely to the myth which (in some versions) states that the corn had twelve ears, although only two showed above the water. In Bitter Water's story Holy Boy succeeded in plucking only the two top ears of the cornstalk before Big Fish attacked him, and that it why the Navaho today put only two ears of corn on each stalk in a sandpainting. We may conclude, therefore, as others have concluded, that the double sandpainting—like many other sandpaintings for which we have records over a long time—exhibits remarkable stability in design over a period of around 50 years. Nevertheless, the variations that do occur are evidence of the lack of "precise standardization" in Navaho ceremonialism (McAllester, 1967, p. 237). The stability manifested in religious affairs is in contrast with the flexibility present in Navaho social organization (Aberle, 1963) and with the changes, especially during the past two decades, in the secular (social and economic) activities attending some ceremonials (Harman, 1964). The lack of standardization, on the other hand, tends toward flexibility, and flexibility of this sort is one of the factors that promotes persistence rather than change (Shepardson and Hammond, 1964, p. 1049).

12. BIG SNAKE PEOPLE

PLATE 17

USNM 377450 (BAE neg. 2457-b-1), 28¾ by 26¾. [OTHER COLLECTIONS: Bush; Reichard. (Ramon Hubbell, Ganado, Arizona, had a painting similar to this one but its present location is unknown.) Paintings of Big Snake People in linear arrangement are in Haile, MNCA, and Bush collections. MNA FILE: SC 129–131. REFERENCES: Newcomb and Reichard, 1937, pp. 53–54, 73, 85, *pl. 8 (color)*; Reichard, 1939, pp. 52–56; Wyman, 1957, pp. 166–176 (Beautyway); 1960, pp. 51–56.]

MAIN THEME CATEGORY.—*Big Snake People.*

DESCRIPTION.—*Radial;* BUWY. *Center:* yellow Snake Peoples' home with red cross (fire) in it. *Main theme symbols:* BUWY Big Snake People, carrying bow and arrow and red tobacco pouch, with their bodies marked with squares (their dens), chevrons (deer or antelope tracks), and curves (phases of the moon) standing on rainbow bars with BUWY crooked snakes (their messengers) at their left. *Quadrants:* black corn, blue beans, white squash, yellow tobacco. *Guardian:* Rainbow. *Paired guardians:* black, white crooked snakes.

This sandpainting commemorates the visit of Holy Man to the home of Big Snake in his *Journey for Knowledge and Power* (see Wyman, 1962, p. 52; Newcomb and Reichard, 1937, p. 33; Reichard, 1939, pp. 51–56; Spencer, 1957, pp. 119–120). In discussing this painting, Bitter Water told Mrs. Newcomb the following story concerning the origin of ceremonial costume and paraphernalia.

In the underworld White Tail-feather and Red Tail-feather (probably Eagle People) gave feathers to Two-faced Woman, and she made headdresses of the red feathers and decorated them with the white ones (today the red cap is made of dyed horsehair). Then she painted half of her hair, face, and body red, the other half black (face and body blackened to match her hair). This woman could walk both ways and look both ways, she looked the same in back as in front. She and her companion had several followers, among them First White, First Blue, and First Yellow. All of these had paint and feather decorations but they were very wicked and started making all sorts of trouble, drinking, gambling, quarreling, adultery, thus starting the evil things that people do today. First Man went to Two-faced Woman and her painted companions to remonstrate. He was very angry. He called all five of them by name. He told Two-faced Woman, the leader, to gather up all the red, white, yellow, blue, and black paint, the red, white, flicker, and turkey feathers, the otter, beaver, mink, and buffalo fur, and the deer and antelope hoof ornaments that made a jingling sound. After she had made a pile of these things, First Man washed all the paint off her face and body with yucca root suds and said, "You shall never wear these things again because you have done nothing but evil things since you have had them." First Man then called a meeting of all the inhabitants of the underworld to decide how the five trouble makers should be punished. They decided to keep all of their ornaments and dress and to take away their powers so that after that they were no more powerful than ordinary people. Then First Man and Fringed Mouth took all the feathers, fur, ornaments, rattles, and incense, and made them into a bundle, and decreed that thereafter any singer who knew the songs, prayers, and ritual of Shootingway could use them for the benefit of the people. The singer hangs a strip of fur around his neck, and uses buffalo fur and hide to make his rattle. Eagle and turkey feathers are tied on the scalp lock with a blue and a white bead. The eagle feather is a prayer feather because the eagle flies highest in the sky, and the turkey feather is a rain feather because the turkey was the last to emerge when the flood drove everyone out of the underworld and his feathers were marked with white foam, yellow pollen, blue rain, and red sunlight. The main part of the feather represents a dark cloud. Twisted cords of beaver or otter skin hang from the wrists and elbows. On their ends are tiny medicine bundles. The tassels on the skirt and the pouch tied to the belt are made of spun cotton and ante-lope hoofs or bits of deer horn are tied to them to make a pleasant noise during the ceremonial.

13. MIXED SNAKE PEOPLE
PLATE 18

USNM 377451 (BAE neg. 2457-b-2), 25 by 25⅝. [OTHER COLLECTIONS: Huckel; Harvey; Stockholm; also, paintings of mixed Snake People in linear arrangement with corn are in the Huckel, Bush, and Stockholm collections. MNA FILE: SC 145–147. REFERENCES: Reichard, 1939, *pl. 14 (color);* also see Newcomb and Reichard, 1937, *pls. 5, 7 (color);* Reichard, 1939, *pl. 16;* and Number 12, above.]

MAIN THEME CATEGORY.—*Mixed Snake People.*

DESCRIPTION.—*Radial;* BUWY. *Center:* black lake (Dark Water; Whisky Creek, Arizona), under which is the Snake Peoples' home. *Main theme symbols:* two pairs of Crooked Snake People—black and white at east, blue and yellow at west (men and women)—and two pairs of Straight Snake People—black and white at south, blue and yellow at north (boys and girls)—carrying bow and arrow and tobacco pouch and standing on rainbow-bars. *Quadrants;* black corn; blue, white, yellow herbs. *Guardian:* Rainbow. *Paired guardians:* black, white crooked snakes.

This sandpainting is also concerned with the visit of the hero to the home of the Snake People (see No. 12). Bitter Water told the following story to account for this sandpainting:

Two children were abducted by the Black Snake People while playing, and taken to the black house under the Dark Water. The Snake People took away their clothing, molded their bodies into snake bodies, and gave them snakeskins to wear. Their parents searched for them and found their footprints leading to the lake. They appealed to the Ye'i for help, so Talking God and Water Sprinkler descended through the lake to the Snake Peoples' house. After asking for the children and being refused four times, Talking God told Black God to intimidate the Snake People with fire [see Wyman, 1962, p. 43]. After four more requests and refusals the fire from Black Gods firedrill became so fierce that the Snake People gave in and brought out the children. Water Sprinkler extinguished the fire, and the three Ye'i took the children home where they were purified in a ceremonial. They had learned all the songs, prayers, and procedure that the Snake People used in their ceremonials, so they became singers of Beautyway and the snake part of Shootingway.

This tale is similar to the major mythic motif *Stolen by Snakes,* of Navaho Windway (see Wyman, 1962, pp. 62, 64).

14. BUFFALO PEOPLE AND HOLY PEOPLE
PLATE 19

USNM 377464 (BAE neg. 2457-b-15), 25½ by 25½. [OTHER COLLECTIONS: Huckel; MNCA; Bush; also, paintings of Buffalo People in linear arrangement are in the Huckel and MNCA collections. MNA FILE: SC 175–179. REFERENCES: Newcomb and Reichard, 1937, pp. 39–40, 47, 63–64, *pl. 28 (color);* Reichard, 1939, pp. 68–73; Haile, 1943, pp. 17, 179–215 (Flintway); Spencer, 1957, pp. 205–207 (Flintway); Wyman 1960, pp. 56–57; 1962, p. 51. Illustrations of paintings of Buffalo People in linear arrangement are in Reichard, 1939, *fig. 9 (line);* Time Magazine, February 23, 1948, *p. 71 (halftone);* also a photograph of an actual sandpainting in use was published in McCombe, 1948, *p. 78,* in Vogt and Kluckhohn, 1951, *p. 38,* and in Wyman, 1960, *fig. 4.*]

MAIN THEME CATEGORY.—*Buffalo People.*

DESCRIPTION.—*Radial;* BUWY. *Center:* yellow house with black border, red cross (fire) in center (the corral where the fire dance is held, according to Judge Yellowhair). *Main theme symbols:* BUWY Buffalo People holding hide rattle, three twigs of spruce (or medicine herbs), feathered travel hoop (magic means of travel); each accompanied by a Holy Person— black Holy Man and Boy (east and south), white Holy Woman and Girl (west and north) wearing variegated dresses—holding hide rattle and spruce or herbs and all standing on rainbow-bars. *Guardian:* Rainbow. *Paired guardians:* black, white Big Fly.

This sandpainting is unique in that it is the only one of its kind recorded in which Buffalo People are accompanied by Holy People. This combination is appropriate, however, because it illustrates the Holy Peoples' *Encounter and Trip with Buffalos* (see Wyman, 1962, p. 51), which is a major motif in the myths of two chantways (see references above). The Buffalo People and Holy People wear Shootingway headdresses and have otter-skin strings and whistles (see No. 1). The Buffalo People have horns, a red-blue lifeline from the heart to the mouth, and a red-blue restoration symbol on the back (see Newcomb and Reichard, 1937, ppl 63–64; Reichard, 1950, p. 681). According to some myths, Buffalo People of this form represent the monstrous children, part human and part buffalo, who were born of the adultery of Holy Man with Buffalo Woman.

15. BUFFALO AND HOMES

PLATE 20

USNM 377469 (BAE neg. 2457–b–20), 34¾ by 32⅛. [OTHER COLLECTIONS: Huckel; Woodard; also, paintings of buffalo, but without their homes, are in the Haile, MNCA, Bush, and Reichard collections. MNA FILE: SC 180–182 (see also, SC 183–188). REFERENCES: Newcomb and Reichard, 1937, pp. 39, 71–72, 78; Reichard, 1939, p. 69, *pl. 23 (color),* cf. Newcomb and Reichard, 1937, *pls. 13, 14–16 (color);* Wyman, 1960, pp. 56–57; also, see No. 14, above.]

ALTERNATIVE TITLE.—The home of the Buffalo People.

MAIN THEME CATEGORY.—*Buffalo.*

DESCRIPTION.—*Radial;* WUYB. *Center:* black lake (Rushing Waters), where the buffalo go to drink, and with rainbow-bars, on which they stand, around it. *Main theme symbols:* WUYB quartets of buffalo, with travel hoops, lifelines, and restoration symbols, and white-black, blue-yellow, yellow-blue, and black-white homes of darkness, day sky, evening twilight, and dawn. *Quadrants:* WUYB medicine herbs. *Guardian:* Mirage or mist garland, with eagle, bluebird (or hawk), red-shafted flicker, and magpie feathers.

The Buffalo People took Holy Man to their home beyond Rushing Waters where Water Monster lived. Judge Yellowhair said that the four kinds of medicine herbs are used for hunters who are hurt while trailing game or who get sick because they have smelled the breath of a dying buffalo, and that the beast's vital parts are in front of the line across the body (restoration symbol). A buffalo cannot be killed by an arrow hitting it behind that line.

16. HOLY PEOPLE OVERCOME BUFFALO

PLATE 21

USNM 377463 (BAE neg. 2457-b-14), 29⅝ by 28½. [OTHER COLLECTIONS: Huckel; Wetherill; Haile; MNCA; Bush; Harvey; ASM. (Ramon Hubbell, Ganado, Arizona, had a painting like this one but its present location is unknown.) MNA FILE: SC 189–199. REFERENCES: Newcomb and Reichard, 1937, pp. 39, 47, 63, *pl. 27 (color);* Reichard, 1939, pp. 70–72, *pl. 24 (color);* Schevill, 1947, *p. 60 (color);* Wyman, 1950, *fig. 1 (halftone);* 1952, p. 35; 1960, pp. 56–57; Spencer, 1957, pp. 206–207.]

ALTERNATIVE TITLES.—Buffalo-who-never-dies, Buffalo People at Jarring Mountain.

MAIN THEME CATEGORY.—*Holy People kill Buffalo.*

DESCRIPTION.—*Radial;* BUWY. *Center:* black lake surrounded by BUWY mountain homes of the Buffalo People (or mountains which Holy Man built to cope with angry buffalo; see Reichard, 1939, p. 70). *Main theme symbols:* Holy Man and Boy and Holy Woman and Girl (as in Nos. 1, 14) holding hide rattle and bow and standing on rainbow-bars; to the left of each a buffalo pierced by an arrow (no restoration symbol). *Quadrants:* black corn, blue beans, black squash, black tobacco. *Guardian:* feathered mirage or mist garland. *Paired guardians:* black, white Big Fly.

The Holy People stand around the lake at jarring mountain, where they killed the Buffalo-who-never-dies. They are about to pull the arrows out of the buffalo and restore them with medicine herbs and songs accompanied by the hide rattle.

17. CORN PEOPLE

PLATE 22

USNM 377459 (BAE neg. 2457-b-10), 16⅝ by 19¾. [OTHER COLLECTIONS: MNCA (copy); Huckel; Wetherill, Bush, Ganado. MNA FILE: SC 201–206. REFERENCES: Newcomb and Reichard, 1937, pp. 38–39, 60, 67, 74, *fig. 10* (*line*), *pl. 21* (*color*): Reichard, 1939, p. 49; Wyman, 1952, pp. 35–36; 1960, p. 50; 1965, *fig. 58* (*halftone*), p. 227 (Red Antway), *figs. 13, 15, 28* (*color illustrations* of actual sandpainting, Red Antway).]

MAIN THEME CATEGORY.—*Corn People.*

DESCRIPTION.—*Linear; UUUU. Main theme symbols:* four dark blue Corn People, hold WYWY (male, female, male, female) ears of corn and baskets (of pollen and dew, or meal); yellow (chin), blue, black, white (forehead) Sun's House stripes face painting (or masks); a bird perches on each center tassel (yellow-headed blackbird, blue swallow, bluebird, yellowbird); a line of yellow pollen runs from beak of each bird to the Corn Person's mouth (song; gift of pollen); a mist of pollen around the corn tassels. *Foundation bar:* the Corn People are rooted in cloud symbols on a black bar of earth with white seeds in it (a long black cloud or the top of a black lake, according to Bitter Water). *Guardian:* Rainbow.

After the Slayer Twins had returned to their mother's home after their visit to their father, the Sun, Changing Woman made this sandpainting as her offering to the Sun (Reichard, 1939, p. 49). In another myth, Holy Man and Holy Boy visited the home of the Corn People and saw this painting, which they took back to Changing Woman's home (Newcomb and Reichard, 1937, p. 38). In still another story, this painting was given to Changing Woman by the Sun. In every instance the painting is associated with Changing Woman.

18. TAIL-FEATHERED ARROW PEOPLE

PLATE 23

USNM 377468 (BAE neg. 2457-b-19), 38⅝ by 37. [OTHER COLLECTIONS: MNCA (copy); Huckel; Bush; Harvey; Ganado; also, paintings of Arrow People in linear arrangement are in Huckel and Haile collections. MNA FILE: SC 208–215. REFERENCES: Newcomb and Reichard, 1937, pp. 36, 50–51, *pl. 35* (*color*); Reichard, 1939, pp. 50–51, *pls. 12, 13* (*color*); Kansas City Times, January 25, 1940, *illustration* (*line*); Spencer, 1957, p. 119; Wyman, 1960, p. 51.]

MAIN THEME CATEGORY.—*Arrow People.*

DESCRIPTION.—*Radial; BYWP. Center:* black mountain, "where the Navaho go to find flints for arrows and weapons" (Judge Yellowhair); lake. *Main theme symbols:* BYWP Tail-feathered Arrow People; eagle-feathered arrow ("white cane"; male), half yellow tail-feathered arrow (eagle, yellow-tailed hawk; female), eagle-feathered "wand" (female), red-feathered "wand" (female); the arms are bows, holding bows and arrows; standing on rainbow-bars and white (eagle), blue, white, red feathers (Sun's jeweled arrows). *Quadrants:* BUWP medicine herbs (used to cure wounds). *Guardian:* Rainbow. *Paired guardians:* Sun, Moon.

This painting was given to Holy Man by the Arrow and Locust People at Emergence Place, where he stole feathers of their sacred black grebe to feather his arrows. It commemorates this event and also the visit of the Holy People to the home of the Arrow People.

Mountain-Shootingway

19. DANCERS WITH SUN, MOON, AND WINDS

PLATE 24

USNM 377470 (BAE neg. 2457–b–21), 37¾ by 36¾. [OTHER COLLECTIONS: MNCA (copy); Newcomb (a painting that is similar to and may have been copied from No. 19). MNA FILE: MSC 5. REFERENCES: Matthews, 1887, pp. 437, 438, 443; Coolidge and Coolidge, 1930, *p. 194* (*a photograph* of two Shootingway dancers costumed like those in this painting); Reagan, 1934, pp. 435, 436, *pl. 8, figs. 1, 2* (*line drawings* of dancers); Haile, 1946, pp. 31, 33–34, 37; Wyman, 1967, pp. 3–5, *fig. 1* (a painting by Big Left-handed of two Shootingway dancers in Mountainway costumed like those in this painting).]

MAIN THEME CATEGORY.—*Dancers.*

Description.—Radial; BUWY. Center: yellow circle with black border, the Dark Circle of Branches (corral), with a red cross (fire) in the center. *Main theme symbols:* BUWY dancers (man, boy, woman, girl) carrying feathered triangular wands and blue Sun with four bluebird feathers (rays), Black Wind with black (magpie) feathers, white Moon with white (eagle) feathers, and Yellow Wind with red (red-shafted flicker) feathers suspended in feathered hoops ("baskets"); all standing on rainbow-bars. *Quadrants:* pairs of tall black-tipped white (eagle), blue (bluebird or blue hawk), white (eagle?), black-tipped red (red-shafted flicker) feathers, each with two white plume feathers on each side of it, standing in blue, yellow, white, and red Navaho baskets (symbolizing the dancing feather act of Mountainway, a Shootingway specialty). *Guardian:* mirage or mist garland: bunches of five white eagle, bluebird or blue hawk, red-shafted flicker, and black magpie feathers at the quadrants. *Paired guardians:* white mountain lion (or wolf), black bear.

The dancers wear Shootingway headdresses to which buffalo horns are attached, and Sun's House stripes face painting (see No. 17); have otter-skin arm strings and collar with attached whistle, and have feathered prayersticks(?) tied to their upper arms. Their bodies are profusely covered with spots of paint.

Dancers such as these present their Shootingway specialty in the Dark Circle of Branches (Corral Dance, Fire Dance) of a Mountainway or Mountain-Shootingway ceremonial. Plate 25 shows four such dancers wearing Shootingway headdresses and carrying (right to left) Sun, Black Wind, Moon, and Yellow Wind symbols like those pictured in the sandpainting (photo taken at the Intertribal Indian Ceremonial, Gallup, New Mexico, about 1935). The magic act known as the dancing feather also is a Shootingway specialty. Dancers attired like those in the painting dance on each side of a Navaho basket in which a tall feather, operated by invisible strings, rises and dances, apparently magically, in time with the dancers' steps.

20. DANCERS WITH SUN, MOON, AND WIND WANDS

PLATE 26

USNM 377457, right half (BAE neg. 2457-b-8, right half). One of two paintings on a piece of cloth that measures 41¾ by 17⅞ inches (the other painting is listed below as Number 24). This painting is unique. [MNA File: MSC 6. References: Matthews, 1887, pp. 437, 438; Haile, 1946, pp. 31, 37; Wyman, 1967, pp. 3–5.]

MAIN THEME CATEGORY.—*Dancers.*

DESCRIPTION.—*Linear:* BWUY. *Main theme symbols:* BWUY dancers carrying long wands with four triangular feathered segments, surmounted by blue Sun, white Moon, Black Wind, or Yellow Wind, and these, in turn, surmounted by cloud symbols with four segments, YUBW (bottom to top), on each of which is perched a bird (yellow-headed blackbird, bluebird with black tail, bluebird, and yellow bird with black head and shoulders and variegated spots). *Guardian:* pink mirage or mist garland; variegated crosses.

The dancers (like those of No. 19) wear Shootingway headdresses with buffalo horns, arm strings, collar, and whistle, but their faces are brown (unmasked, unpainted) and there are no spots on their bodies. Their collars and whistles are especially elaborate. Bitter Water called them Buffalo People. Like the dancers in Number 19 they are depicted

presenting a Shootingway specialty in the corral dance of a Mountainway or Mountain-Shootingway ceremonial. Four such dancers carrying Sun, Moon, and Wind wands like those pictured in the sandpainting, are shown in Plate 27 (a photo taken at the Intertribal Indian Ceremonial, Gallup, New Mexico, about 1935).

21. DANCERS WITH CACTUS

PLATE 28

USNM 377458 (BAE neg. 2457–b–9), 17⅝ by 23¾. This painting is unique. [MNA File: MSC 7. References: Reagan, 1934, p. 436, *pl. 8, fig. 3;* Haile, 1946, pp. 47–48; Kluckhohn and Wyman, 1940, pp. 133–134, *figs. 16, 17* (Navaho Windway); Wyman, 1962, pp. 308–309, *figs. 49–51* (Navaho Windway).]

MAIN THEME CATEGORY.—*Dancers.*

DESCRIPTION.—*Linear;* BWUY or WBYU. *Main theme symbols:* two pairs of dancers (each pair approaching a cactus plant), carrying BUYP water jugs (rain rattles or rain makers—Horse Herder) and black cloud symbols attached to black-white crooked male lightnings or red-blue straight female lightnings. *Guardian:* yellow-white straight (female) lightning. *Paired guardians:* white-black and white-yellow crooked (male) lightning.

The east and south dancers, male and female, have bodies that are white above and black below (or the reverse, respectively), and they approach a black cactus rooted in a black pool with a crooked white lightning running lengthwise on it (the path of the rising sap). The west and north dancers, male and female, have bodies that are yellow above and blue below (or the reverse) and they approach a dark blue cactus. These blue cactus plants are used for a male patient; white and yellow plants would be used for a female.

Cactus plants and Cactus People are characteristic of the sandpaintings of the Windways (see Kluckhohn and Wyman, 1940, and Wyman, 1962, in the references above). Moreover, Horse Herder (of Chinle, Arizona) and Wind Chanter (of Sweetwater, Arizona) assigned this sandpainting to Navaho Windway. When the First People were moving out of the underworld they found nothing to eat when they came to the wide deserts, so the Cactus People showed them how to use cactus for food, and the Wind told them how to prepare it and warned them against certain poisonous plants; so, cactus and the Cactus People are now remembered in the Wind Chant (Wind Chanter; see Wyman and Kluckhohn, 1938, p. 13, footnote 30, for another explanation). Because the People in this sandpainting wear Shootingway head-dresses and because lightning guardians are present, it seems likely that it is a representation of dancers performing with cactus in the corral dance of a Mountainway or Mountain-Shootingway. In 1923 Reagan (1934, p. 436) saw "cactus actors" carrying "sticks three feet long to which 'finger' cactus was profusely tied . . . who danced facing each other" in a corral dance of a Mountainway at Steamboat Rock, Arizona. Moreover, Father Berard Haile (1946, pp. 47–48) stated that although "Navaho Windway and Chiricahua Windway were also not invited, because the singer considered winds injurious . . . other singers, however, are now allowing Navaho Windway singers to exhibit cactus bunches, a girl dancer, and a group of four men and four women dancers." It seems safe, therefore, to assign this sandpainting to Mountain-Shootingway.

22. DANCERS WITH LIGHTNINGS

PLATE 29

USNM 377456 (BAE neg. 2457–b–7), 24¾ by 28⅝. This painting is unique, but there is a copy in MNCA and a copy in ASM. [MNA FILE: MSC 8. REFERENCE: Reagan, 1934, p. 436, *pl. 8, fig. 4.*]

ALTERNATIVE TITLE.—Cloud, water, and arrow sandpainting (Bitter Water).

MAIN THEME CATEGORY.—*Dancers.*

DESCRIPTION.—*Radial*; BWUY. *Center:* black lake. *Main theme symbols:* BWYU dancers (Dragon Fly People—Bitter Water) carrying twined (flash) lightnings, in each hand, and a water jug (rain rattle) and surrounded by lightnings, sunrays, or rainbows. *Quadrants:* BYUY Cloud People with lightnings, etc., protruding from the corners of their four segments. *Guardian:* white-black crooked lightning.

Shafts of black-white crooked male lightning in the eastern person's hands have their points in the central lake, and similar shafts run from his feet to cross over his head. White-yellow crooked sunrays surround the southern person and blue-red(?) straight female lightnings and red-blue straight (female) rainbows surround the southern, western, and northern persons. Corresponding lightnings sunrays, or rainbows come from the Cloud People. The twined lightnings which the people carry are lightning sticks, built like lazy tongs, that can open and close.

This sandpainting represents a Shootingway specialty which may be presented in the corral dance of a Mountainway or Mountain-Shootingway ceremonial. Reagan (1934, p. 436) described such an act that he witnessed in 1923:

Lightning was represented in the dance that followed by lazy tongs which the special actors carried in front of them. This device, when pressed, would plunge forward some eight or ten feet. At every turn at every gesture-position in the song, and when presented to the fire as a closing act, it was thrust foward while its bearer posed in strutting posture. These actions were repeated many times.

A manuscript (M–3 in MNCA) containing a description of a Male Mountainway ceremonial given by John Sherman at Saw Mill, north of Fort Defiance, Arizona, on November 17, 1951, has the following statement: "They said also, they gave the lightning dance where four men carry sticks which they shot out over the fire and over the patients."

Big Starway

Big Starway is an uncommon (perhaps obsolescent) ceremonial which today usually is performed according to Evilway ritual. It seems certain, however, that there is or has been a Holyway form of the chant. Big Starway Evilway is used to alleviate troubles attributed to the evil influences of the ghosts of Navahos or to witchcraft. Among these conditions are bad dreams, insomnia, fainting, nervousness, mental disturbances, or almost any ailment thought to be caused by native ghosts or witches. Any Evilway ceremonial may be used for similar purposes. The sandpaintings of Big Starway, as might be expected, feature stars—either alone or in combination with Star People, the Slayer Twins, Earth and Sky, Thunders, Cloud People, snakes of various kinds, Big Flies, or mountains.

23. STAR PEOPLE AND ENDLESS SNAKE

PLATE 30

USNM 377461 (BAE neg. 2457–b–12), 19¾ by 22⅝. [OTHER COLLECTIONS: MNCA (copy); Reichard. MNA FILE: BSC 5, 6. REFERENCES: Reichard, 1950, pp. 696, 698, *fig. 19 (line)*; see Wheelwright, 1956, for myth.]

MAIN THEME CATEGORY.—*People.*

DESCRIPTION.—*Radial;* BUYW. *Center:* Black Star. *Main theme symbols:* BUYW flint-armored Star People, each carrying a bow and arrow and wearing a bandoleer (or quiver). *Guardian:* Black Endless Snake, with four coils in each quadrant.

Snakes are prominent in the myth and in some of the sandpaintings of Big Starway (see Wheelwright, 1956). According to Slim White, the coils at the quadrants of the Endless Snake guardian are "to raise the mountains up from the ground." This singer said that when he makes this sandpainting the coils are made around the four sacred mountains and that two little stars are used for paired guardians. On the first day the snake is black, and on the second, third, and fourth days it is blue, yellow, and white, respectively. This painting may be used for the Evil-way ritual. The principal sandpaintings are made in the evening, and the patient sleeps on some of the sand all night (see Reichard, 1950, p. 696). Black God gave star knowledge to earth people.

Beautyway

Beautyway and Mountainway are related ceremonials in that their myths branch off from a single legend. Beautyway is used to cure a wide variety of diseases attributed to improper contact with snakes, bad dreams about snakes, or even snake bite. Snakes and Snake People are prominent in the myth and in the sandpaintings as well as in the etiology of the chant. English-speaking Navahos sometimes refer to Beauty-way as the "Snake Chant." The sandpaintings of Beautyway have been thoroughly described, analyzed, and illustrated by Wyman (1957) and Wyman and Newcomb (1962).

24. BEAUTYWAY DANCERS IN MOUNTAIN-WAY

PLATE 31

USNM 377457, left half (BAE neg. 2457–b–8, left half). This is one of two paintings on a piece of cloth that measures 41¾ by 17⅞ inches; the other is number 20. This painting is unique, but a copy is in the New-comb collection. [MNA FILE: BTC 12, 12A. REFERENCES: Matthews, 1887, 437–438; Wyman, 1957, pp. 165–166, 176–177, 183, 184; Wyman and Newcomb, 1962, p. 39, *fig. 1 (halftone).*]

ALTERNATIVE TITLES.—People of the myth with feathers [arcs]; Dance of the standing arcs.

MAIN THEME CATEGORY.—*People of the myth.*

DESCRIPTION.—*Linear; BUYW. Main theme symbols:* BUYW dancers wearing headdresses of a rainbow arc bearing twelve black-tipped white eagle feathers and subtended by a white cord, white face paintings or masks, otter skin collars with an attached whistle (very ornate), and white-yellow arm strings (otter skin?); they carry three green sprigs of spruce(?) in each hand. *Guardian:* white-black crooked lightning. *Paired guardians:* crossed black and blue crooked snakes on blue Sun, yellow and white crooked snakes on white Moon.

This sandpainting represents Beautyway dancers performing the dance of the standing arcs as described by Matthews (1887) in the Dark Circle of Branches of a Mountainway ceremonial. The reasons for such identification are discussed in Wyman and

Newcomb (1962). Whether this sandpainting would be used in a Mountainway chant or in a Beautyway chant, or in both, is not known. The feathered arcs in this painting are reminiscent of those in a Navaho Windway painting of Wind People with feathers and corn, but otherwise the two are entirely different.

25. PEOPLE OF THE MYTH

PLATE 32

USNM 377471 (BAE neg. 2457–b–22), 36¾ by 36¾. [There are no other sandpaintings like this one on record, but paintings of People of the Myth in radial compositions are in the Wetherill, MNCA, Newcomb, Oakes, and Stockholm collections. MNA FILE: BTC 13–25. REFERENCES: Wyman, 1957, pp. 161, 165–166, 176–177, 183, 184, *fig. 6 (line), pl. 9 (color);* Wyman and Newcomb, 1962, pp. 39–42, *fig. 2 (halftone).*]

ALTERNATIVE TITLE.—Snake People.

MAIN THEME CATEGORY.—*People of the myth.*

DESCRIPTION.—*Radial.* Since there are no clues to orient this painting, the directional color sequence is problematical. The following description gives a possible orientation. *Center:* black pool(?) surrounded by yellow squash(?) blossoms. *Main theme symbols:* pairs of Snake(?) People—two black and blue, two white and yellow—wearing weasel or tall feather headdresses, white face painting or masks, otter-skin arm strings and collars with ornate whistle attached; holding two eagle feathers and three blue sprigs of some kind of plant; and standing on rainbow-bars. *Quadrants:* UBWY medicine plants. There are no guardians, but there are five feathers—yellow-tipped blue, black-tipped white (eagle), black-tipped red (red-shafted flicker), and blue-tipped yellow—in the quadrants outside of the medicine plants.

Nightway

The Night Chant, along with the Mountain Chant, is one of the Navaho ceremonials best known to non-Navahos. Contributing to its fame are the spectacular dances of the final night performed by masked impersonators of supernatural beings; the peculiar, stirring singing accompanying the dances (which are often selected for public exhibitions outside of ceremonial practice); and the fact that some of the first substantial descriptions of a Navaho ceremonial were devoted to this chant. Nightway is considered to be an efficacious cure for all sorts of head ailments—including eye and ear diseases and mental derangements—but it may be used for other conditions, such as gastrointestinal diseases, if such ailments are attributed to the proper etiological factors. The sandpaintings of Nightway are mostly concerned with various combinations of members of the class of supernaturals known as the Ye'i. As mentioned above, they have been described and illustrated in several early publications (Stevenson, 1891; Matthews, 1902; Tozzer, 1909).

26. FIRST DANCERS

Plate 33

USNM 377454 (BAE neg. 2457-b-5), 26⅝ by 24½. [Other Collections: Wetherill; MNA (Euler); also, paintings of First Dancers in linear arrangement are in the Bush, Haile, and ASM collections. MNA File: NC 19–22. References: No illustrations of this radial-composition sandpainting are known to have been published, but illustrations of paintings of First Dancers in linear arrangement are indicated in some of the following references: Stevenson, 1891, pp. 263–265, 273–275, *pl. 122 (color);* Matthews, 1902, pp. 128–129, *pl. 7 (color);* Tozzer, 1909, pp. 326–327, *pl. 3 (halftone);* Haile, 1947a, pp. 16, 18–20, 31, 73–75; Wyman, 1952, pp. 84–85.]

ALTERNATIVE TITLE.—Dancing group.

MAIN THEME CATEGORY.—*First Dancers.*

DESCRIPTION.—*Radial. Center:* black lake (near the home of the Ye'i). *Main theme symbols:* four quartets of two black Male and two blue Female Gods, alternating, standing on rainbow-bars. All wear blue face masks. Each Male God has a round mask, with two black-tipped white eagle feathers and black-spotted yellow fluffy owl feathers at their base attached to its left side, and carries a white gourd and three blue sprigs of spruce. Female Gods have rectangular masks and carry spruce twigs in both hands. *Quadrants:* white corn, blue beans, black squash, blue tobacco. *Guardian:* Rainbow.

Masked impersonators of Male and Female Gods (Ye'i) appear in dances performed on the ninth night of the Night Chant. This public exhibition is often called the *Ye'i bichai* dance, although this name, which means maternal grandfather of the Ye'i, is properly a name used for Talking God, the leader of the Ye'i (see Matthews, 1902, pp. 146–151). Big Lefthanded painted two realistic pictures of the *Ye'i bichai* dancers of Nightway (USNM 377477, 377479) which, together with three other of his secular paintings, have been described by Wyman (1967, figs. 2, 4).

Plumeway

Plumeway, also known as Downway or the Feather Chant, is related to Nightway. Masked impersonators

of the Ye'i perform in both chants, and representations of them appear in the sandpaintings of both. Plumeway (an uncommon ceremonial) is used, like Nightway, for diseases of the head or other ailments when these are attributed to infection from game animals, especially deer. Such troubles may be called "deer disease." Game and hunting are emphasized in the myth, and many of the sandpaintings contain representations of deer or other wild animals. The origins of agriculture also are stressed, both in the myth and the sandpaintings.

27. THE FARM

Plate 34

USNM 377466 (BAE neg. 2457–b–17), 22½ by 21¾. [Other Collections: MNCA (including a copy), ASM (copy); Newcomb. MNA File: PC 56–58. References: Matthews, 1897, pp. 172–173, 181–185; 1902, pp. 187–193 (Nightway); Goddard, 1933, pp. 161–163; Sapir and Hoijer, 1942, pp. 28–29; Wheelwright, 1946a, pp. 74–75, 94 (Waterway); Wyman, 1952, p. 88; Spencer, 1957, pp. 169–172, 175.]

ALTERNATIVE TITLES.—Food plants and animals; game animals and plants.

MAIN THEME CATEGORY.—*Corn with animals.*

DESCRIPTION.—*Radial; BUYW. Center:* black lake. *Main theme symbols:* black, blue, yellow corn, white squash; twelve pairs of game animals with males on left side of plants and females on the right side; black male and blue female deer (inside), yellow antelope (middle), black male and blue female mountain sheep (outside). (Two pairs of mountain sheep are reversed; one animal is missing; and one is misplaced.) *Quadrants:* BUYW wild food plants (deer food), such as Rocky Mountain bee balm (or beans?), pigweed, etc. All plants are rooted in two-tiered cloud symbols. *Guardian:* Rainbow.

This sandpainting illustrates two episodes in the myth of Plumeway. The hero, having floated down the San Juan River in a hollow log, assisted by the Ye'i, lands and plants a field of corn and other domesticated plants (the farm) with seeds provided by his pet turkey. Then he marries Deer Owner's daughter, introduces his new relatives to corn, and is shown various kinds of game animals which his father-in-law keeps in an underground game farm. A much more complicated version (in Newcomb collection) by Plumeway Singer (Canyon People's Son) of White Cone, Arizona has 64 animals (including the turkey) in the quadrants; and a simpler version (in MNCA, and possibly by the same singer) has only four pairs of deer. Many of the sandpaintings of Plumeway contain turkeys and/or numerous wild animals of various kinds (see Reichard, 1950, pp. 699–703, figs. 20–22).

Navaho Windway

Navaho Windway is used to treat any disease attributed to the influence of winds, snakes or lightning, or cactus. The list of ailments that may be ascribed to these factors is a long one (see Wyman, 1962, pp. 20–22), but stomach trouble (snake infection), skin diseases and eye trouble (cactus infection), and heart and lung diseases are often mentioned. The sandpaintings of the Windways of the Navaho are described, analyzed, and illustrated by Wyman (1962).

28. WIND PEOPLE DRESSED IN SNAKES

Plate 35

USNM 377467 (BAE neg. 2457–b–18), 24⅞ by 28½. [Other Collections: Huckel; MNCA; Bush; Newcomb; Reichard; ASM; Dendahl. MNA File: NWC 19–33. References: Kluckhohn and Wyman, 1940, pp. 132–133, *pl. 6, fig. 15 (halftone);* Dutton, 1941, pp. 77–78, *illustration on p. 79 (halftone);* Wheelwright, 1946, pp. 1–5; Wyman, 1960, pp. 72–73; 1962, pp. 292, 297–299, *figs. 10 (line), 11 (color).*]

Main theme category.—*Wind People dressed in snakes.*

Description.—*Linear;* BUYW (north to south; see Wyman, 1962, p. 285). *Main theme symbols:* BUYW flint-armored Wind People, standing on Big Snakes, carry crooked snakes in both hands and have crooked snakes instead of arm strings, two crooked snakes crossed over their waists and two projecting from their knees and ankles. *Guardian:* Rainbow. *Paired guardians:* blue, black crooked snakes.

Since *Stolen by Snakes, Snake Transformation,* and *Snake Marriage* are major mythic motifs of Navaho Windway (see Wyman, 1962, pp. 60–64, 69–71, 75–76), it is appropriate that Wind People are depicted with snakes in sandpaintings (see Wyman, 1962, pp. 289–292). Sixty-six of 133 Navaho Windway sandpaintings involve snakes in one way or another (see Wyman, 1962, p. 290, table 9). Horse Herder told Mrs. Newcomb that the Wind People carry snakes everywhere they go, and that is why there are more snakes in the low country, where the wind blows all the time, than on the mountains, where it blows only part of the time; that the Wind People live in the same caves in which the snakes hibernate; and that the Big Snakes (under the feet of the Wind People) never leave their cave homes.

Literature Cited

Aberle, David F.
1963. Some sources of Flexibility in Navaho Social Organization. *Southwestern Journal of Anthropology*, 19:1–8.
1966. The Peyote Religion among the Navaho. *Viking Fund Publications in Anthropology*, Number 42. Wenner-Gren Foundation for Anthropological Research.

Boyd, Phyllis J.
1953. Sand-Painting Doctor. *Family Circle*, 43:84–89.

Coolidge, Dane, and Mary R. Coolidge
1930. The Navajo Indians. Boston: Houghton Mifflin Company.

Douglas, Frederic H., and Rene D'Harnoncourt
1941. Indian Art of the United States. New York: The Museum of Modern Art.

Dutton, Bertha P.
1941. The Navaho Wind Way Ceremonial. *El Palacio*, 48: 73–82.

Foster, Kenneth E.
1964. Navajo sandpaintings. *Navajoland Publications*, series 3, Window Rock, Arizona: Navajo Tribal Museum.

Goddard, Pliny Earle
1933. Navajo Texts. *Anthropological Papers of the American Museum of Natural History*, 34(1):127–179.

Haile, Father Berard
1943. Origin Legend of the Navaho Flintway. *University of Chicago Publications in Anthropology, Linguistic Series*.
1946. The Navaho Fire Dance. Saint Michaels, Arizona: St. Michaels Press.
1947. Starlore among the Navaho. Santa Fe, New Mexico: Museum of Navajo Ceremonial Art.
1947a. Head and Face Masks in Navaho Ceremonialism. Saint Michaels, Arizona: St. Michaels Press.
1947b. Prayerstick Cutting in a Five Night Ceremonial of the Male Branch of Shootingway. Chicago: University of Chicago Press.
1950. Legend of the Ghostway Ritual in the Male Branch of Shootingway. Saint Michaels, Arizona: St. Michaels Press.

Harman, Robert
1964. Change in a Navajo Ceremonial. *El Palacio*, 71:20–26.

Kluckhohn, Clyde
1960. Navaho Categories. *In*, Culture in History (Stanley Diamond, editor), pages 65–98. New York: Columbia University Press.

Kluckhohn, Clyde, and Leland C. Wyman
1940. An Introduction to Navaho Chant Practice. *American Anthropological Association Memoir*, Number 53.

Leighton, Alexander H., and Dorothea Leighton
1944. The Navaho Door. Cambridge: Harvard University Press.

Matthews, Washington
1887. The Mountain Chant: A Navajo Ceremony. *Fifth Annual Report, Bureau of American Ethnology*, pages 379–467.
1897. Navaho Legends. *Memoirs, American Folklore Society*, Volume 5.
1902. The Night Chant. *Memoirs, American Museum of Natural History*, Volume 6.

McAllester, David P.
1967. Review of "The Red Antway of the Navaho" by Leland C. Wyman. *American Anthropologist*, 69: 237–238.

McCombe, Leonard
1948. The Navajos. *Life Magazine*, 24:75–83.

Mills, George
1959. Navaho Art and Culture. Colorado Springs: The Taylor Museum, Colorado Springs Fine Arts Center.

Mullen, Read
1964. Read Mullen Gallery of Western Art, Catalog. Phoenix, Arizona.

Newcomb, Franc J.
1931. Description of the Symbolism of a Sand-Painting of the Sun. *In*, Introduction to American Indian Art. Part 2, pages 8–9. New York: The Exposition of Indian Tribal Arts, Inc.
1936. Symbols in Sand. *New Mexico Magazine*, 14 : 24–25.
1940. Navajo Omens and Taboos. Santa Fe, New Mexico: The Rydal Press.

Newcomb, Franc J.; Stanley Fishler and Mary C. Wheelwright
1956. A Study of Navajo Symbolism. *Papers of the Peabody Museum, Harvard University*, 32 : (3).

Newcomb, Franc J., and Gladys A. Reichard
1937. Sandpaintings of the Navajo Shooting Chant. New York: J. J. Augustin.

Oakes, Maud; Joseph Campbell; and Jeff King
1943. Where the Two Came to Their Father. *Bollingen Series*, Number 1. New York: Pantheon Books.

O'Bryan, Aileen
1956. The Díné: Origin Myths of the Navaho Indians. *Bureau of American Ethnology Bulletin*, 163.

Oehser, Paul H.
1949. Sons of Science: The Story of the Smithsonian Institution and Its Leaders. New York: Henry Schuman.

Reagan, Albert B.
1934. A Navaho Fire Dance. *American Anthropologist*, 36 : 434–437.

Reichard, Gladys A.
1934. Spider Woman. New York: Macmillan Company.
1936. Navajo Sheperd and Weaver. New York: J. J. Augustin.
1939. Navajo Medicine Man. New York: J. J. Augustin.
1950. Navaho Religion: A Study of Symbolism. *Bollingen Series*, Number 18. New York: Pantheon Books.

Sapir, Edward, and Harry Hoijer
1942. Navaho Texts. Iowa City: Linguistic Society of America.

Schevill, Margaret E.
1945. The Navajo Screen. *The Kiva*, 11:3–5.
1947. Beautiful on the Earth. Santa Fe, New Mexico: Hazel Dreis Editions.

Shepardson, Mary, and Blodwen Hammond
1964. Change and Persistence in an Isolated Navajo Community. *American Anthropologist*, 66:1029–1050.

Sloan, John, and Oliver LaFarge
1931. Introduction to American Indian Art. Part 1. New York: The Exposition of Indian Tribal Arts, Inc.

Spencer, Katherine
1957. Mythology and Values: An Analysis of Navaho Chantway Myths. *Memoirs, American Folklore Society*, Volume 48.

Stevenson, James
1891. Ceremonial of Hasjelti Dailjis. *Eighth Annual Report, Bureau of American Ethnology*, pages 229–285.

Tanner, Clara Lee
1964. Modern Navajo Weaving. *Arizona Highways*, 40:6–19.

Tozzer, Alfred M.
1909. Notes on Religious Ceremonies of the Navaho. Putnam Anniversary Volume, pages 299–343. New York and Cedar Rapids.

Vogt, Evon Z., and Clyde Kluckhohn
1951. Navaho Means People. Cambridge, Massachusetts: Harvard University Press.

Watkins, Frances E.
1943. The Navaho. *Southwest Museum Leaflets*, Number 16.

Wheelwright, Mary C.
1946. Wind Chant and Feather Chant. *Museum of Navajo Ceremonial Art Bulletin*, 4.
1946a. Hail Chant and Water Chant. Santa Fe, New Mexico: Museum of Navajo Ceremonial Art.
1949. Emergence Myth. Santa Fe, New Mexico: Museum of Navajo Ceremonial Art.
1956. The Great Star Chant. Santa Fe, New Mexico: Museum of Navajo Ceremonial Art.
1958. Myth of Willa-chee-ji Deginnh-keygo Hatral (Holy Form of the Red Ant Chant). *Museum of Navajo Ceremonial Art Bulletin*, 7.

Wyman, Leland C.
1950. The Religion of the Navaho Indians. *In*, Forgotten Religions (Virgilius Ferm, editor), pages 341–361. New York: The Philosophical Library.
1952. The Sandpaintings of the Kayenta Navaho. *University of New Mexico Publications in Anthropology*, Number 7.
1957. Beautyway: A Navaho Ceremonial. *Bollingen Series*, Number 53. New York: Pantheon Books.
1959. Navaho Indian Painting: symbolism, artistry, and psychology. Boston: Boston University Press.
1960. Navaho Sandpainting: The Huckel Collection. Colorado Springs: The Taylor Museum, Colorado Springs Fine Arts Center.
1962. The Windways of the Navaho. Colorado Springs: The Taylor Museum, Colorado Springs Fine Arts Center.
1965. The Red Antway of the Navaho. Santa Fe, New Mexico: Museum of Navajo Ceremonial Art.
1967. Big Lefthanded, Pioneer Navajo artist. *Plateau*, 40 : 1–13.
1967a. The Sacred Mountains of the Navaho. Flagstaff, Arizona: Museum of Northern Arizona, Northland Press.
1970. Blessingway. Tucson: University of Arizona Press.

Wyman, Leland C., and Flora L. Bailey
1964. Navaho Indian Ethnoentomology. *University of New Mexico Bulletin*, 366.

Wyman, Leland C., and Clyde Kluckhohn
1938. Navaho Classification of Their Song Ceremonials. *American Anthropological Association Memoir*, Number 50.

Wyman, Leland C., and Franc J. Newcomb
1962. Sandpaintings of Beautyway. *Plateau*, 35 : 37–52.
1963. Drypaintings Used in Divination by the Navajo. *Plateau*, 36:18–24.

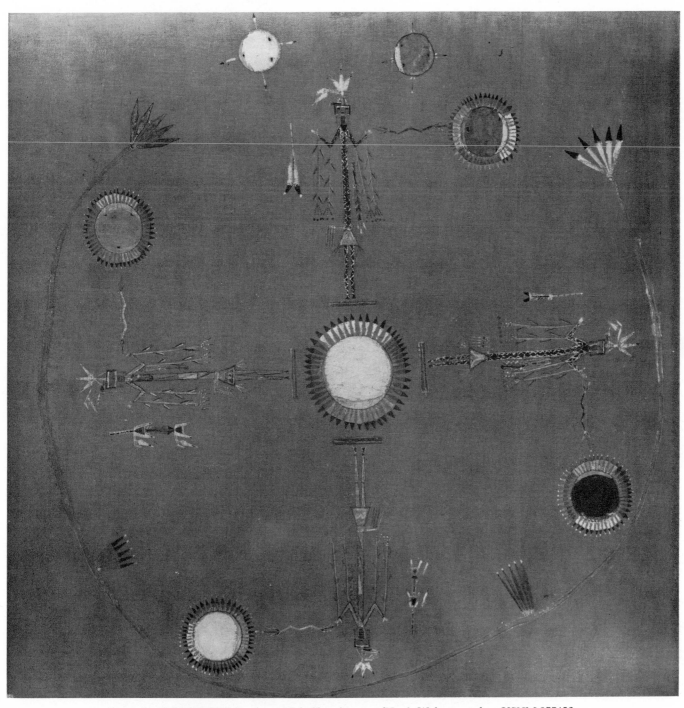

PLATE 1.—Whirling Tail Feathers, Male Shootingway. (No. 1, Walcott catalog; USNM 377453; BAE negative 2457–b–4.)

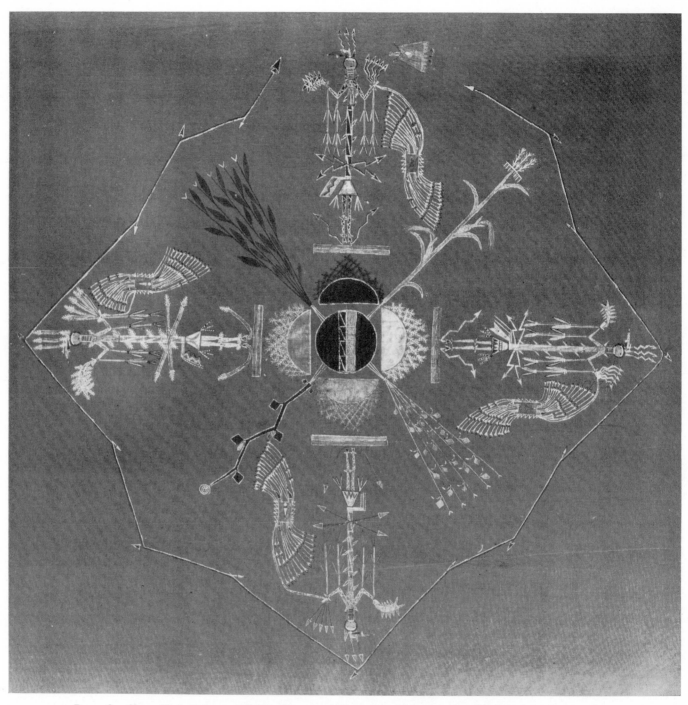

PLATE 2.—Slayer Twin Quartet with Flint House and Mountains, Male Shootingway. (No. 2, Walcott catalog; USNM 377452; BAE negative 2457–b–3.)

PLATE 3.—Earth and Sky, Male Shootingway. (No. 3, Walcott catalog; USNM 377460; BAE negative 2457–b–11.)

PLATE 4.—The Skies, Male Shootingway. (No. 4, Walcott catalog; USNM 377455; BAE negative 2457–b–6.)

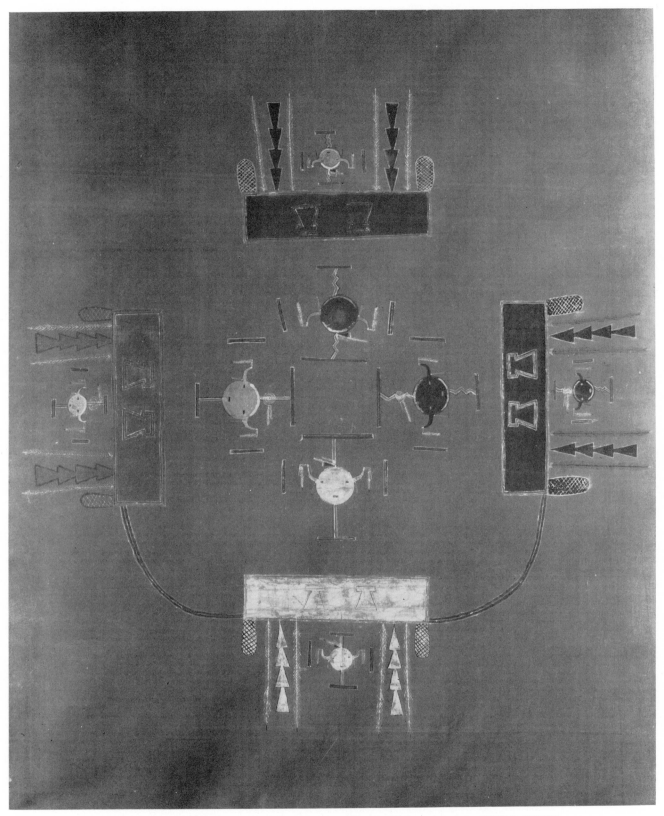

PLATE 5.—Cloud Houses, Male Shootingway. (No. 5, Walcott catalog; USNM 377472; BAE negative 2457–b–23.)

56

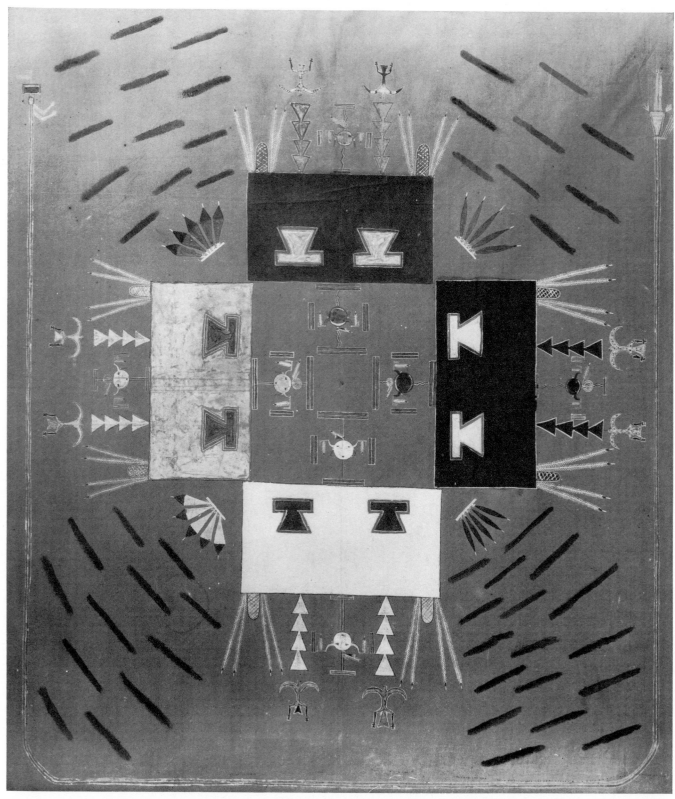

Plate 6.—Cloud Houses, Male Shootingway. (No. 6, Walcott catalog; USNM 377475; BAE negative 2457–b–26.)

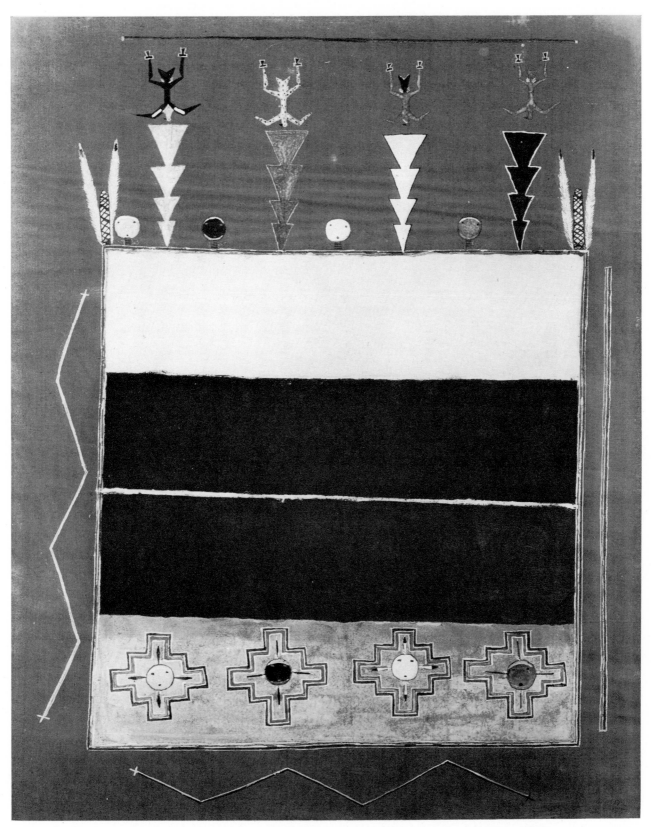

PLATE 7.—Sun's House, Male Shootingway. (No. 7, Walcott catalog; USNM 377462; BAE negative 2457–b–13.)

58

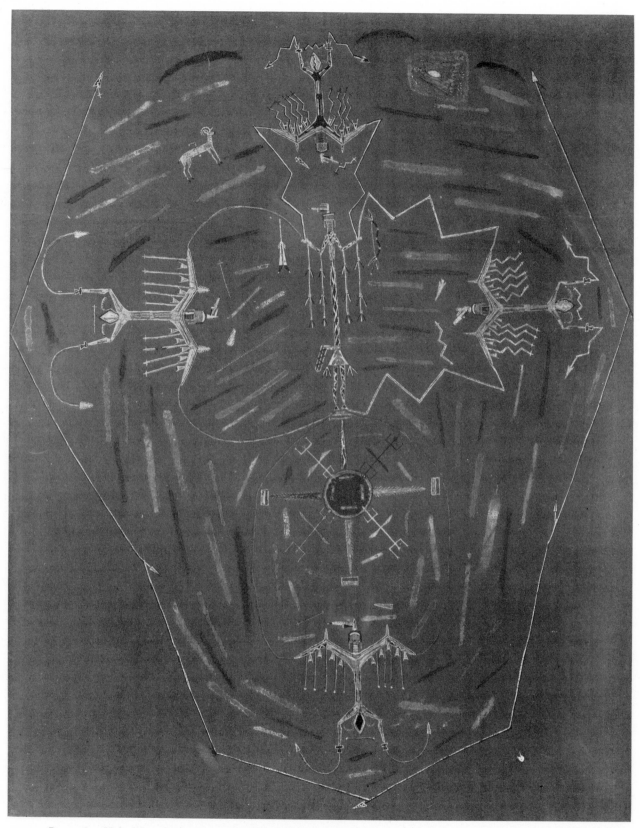

PLATE 8.—Holy Man Captured by Thunders, Male Shootingway. (No. 9, Walcott catalog; USNM 377465; BAE negative 2457–b–16.)

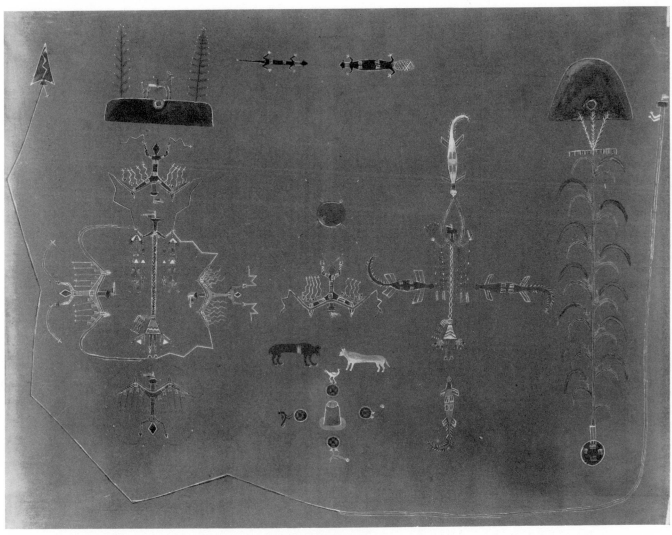

PLATE 9.—Sky-reaching Rock, Male Shootingway. (No. 10, Walcott catalog; USNM 377473; BAE negative 2457–b–24.)

PLATE 10.—Portion of the double sandpainting showing the center with Sky-reaching Rock represented by a tall cone of clay and part of the southern composition, Swallowed by Fish, and, in the background, the bottom of the Sun's House screen (see Walcott catalog, No. 7). Photograph taken by Katherine Harvey at an actual ceremonial, presumably near Kayenta, Arizona, about 1930. (Courtesy Museum of Northern Arizona.)

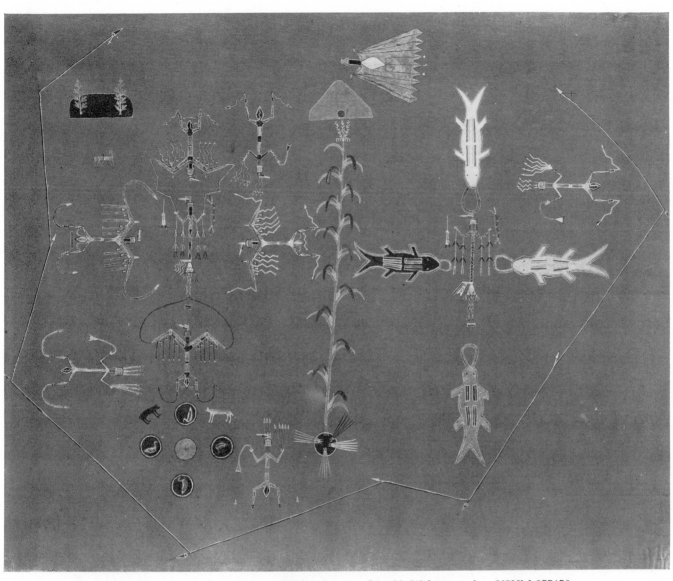

PLATE 11.—Sky-reaching Rock, Male Shootingway. (No. 11, Walcott catalog; USNM 377476; BAE negative 2457–b–27.)

62

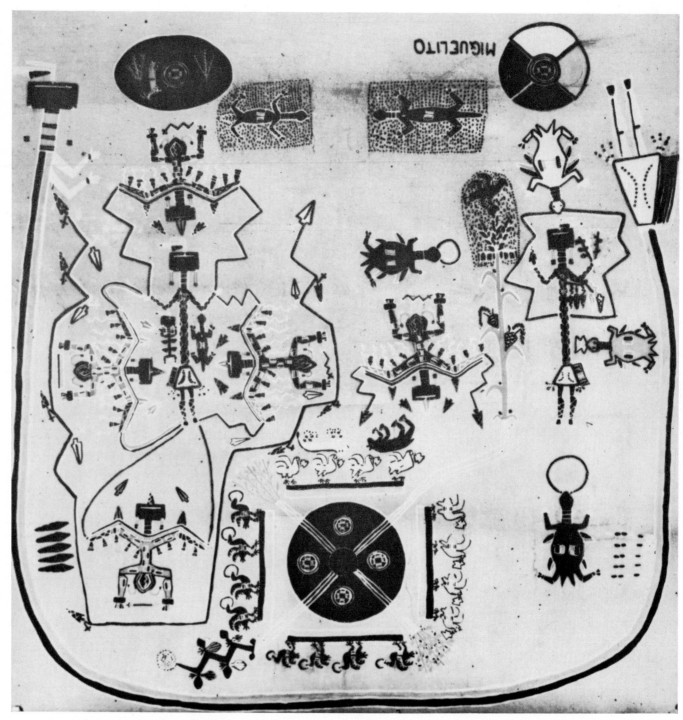

PLATE 12.—Sky-reaching Rock, Male Shootingway. Painting made by Red Point (Miguelito), near Ganado, Arizona; collected by Nils Hogner, 1929 or 1930. (Courtesy Etnografiska Museet, Stockholm, Sweden.)

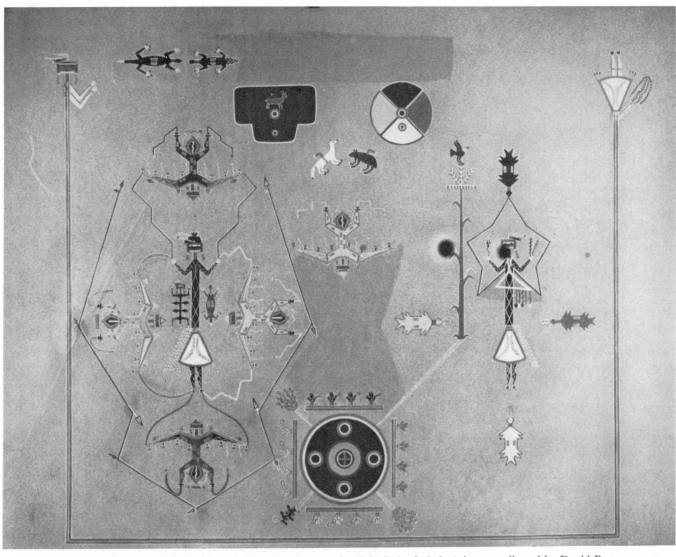

PLATE 13.—Sky-reaching Rock, Male Shootingway, by RC, Lukachukai, Arizona; collected by David P. McAllester, 1957. (Courtesy Museum of Navaho Ceremonial Art.)

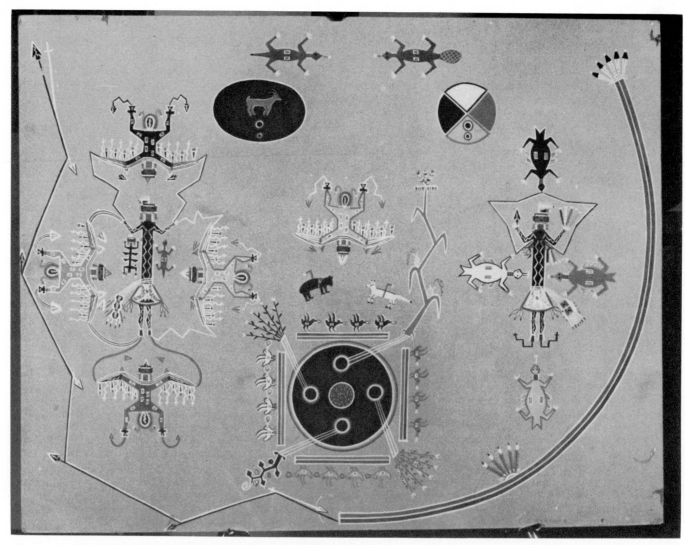

PLATE 14.—Sky-reaching Rock, Male Shootingway, by Blue Eyes' nephew, Newcomb, New Mexico; recorded by Franc J. Newcomb before 1930. (Courtesy Museum of Navaho Ceremonial Art.)

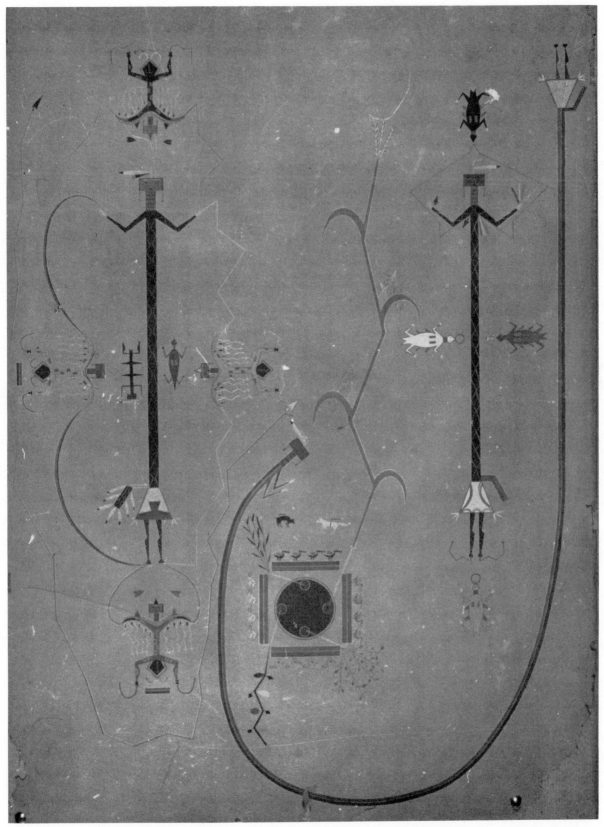

PLATE 15.—Sky-reaching Rock, Male Shootingway, by Yellow Singer (Sam Chief), Oljeto, Utah; collected by Louisa Wade Wetherill between 1910 and 1918. (Courtesy Museum of Northern Arizona.)

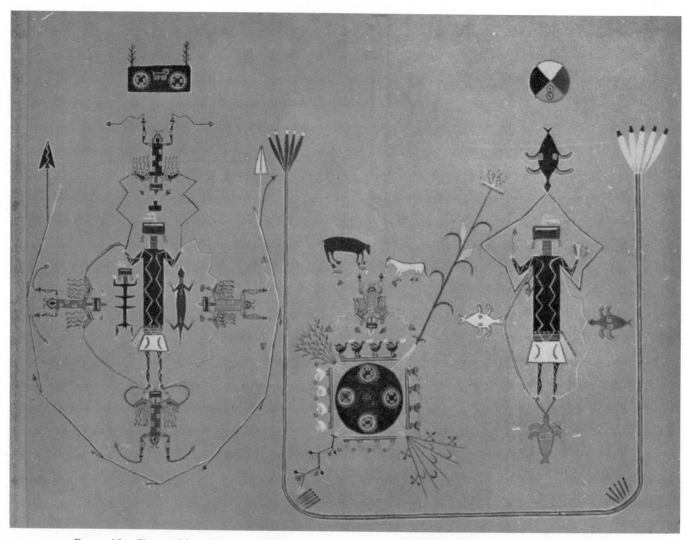

PLATE 16.—Sky-reaching Rock, Male Shootingway by Gray Man, Chinle Wash, Arizona; collected by Father Berard Haile in 1934. (Courtesy Museum of Northern Arizona.)

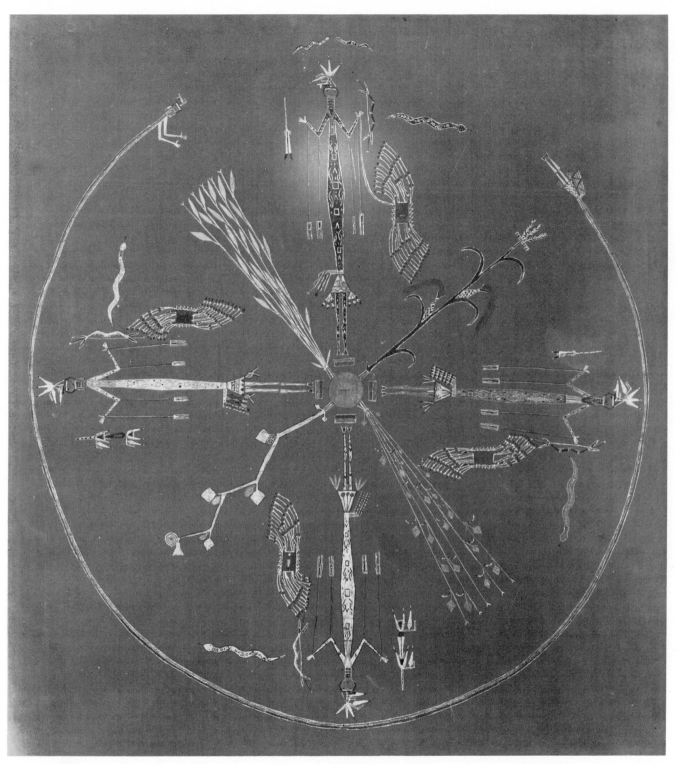

PLATE 17.—Big Snake People, Male Shootingway. (No. 12, Walcott catalog; USNM 377450; BAE negative 2457-b-1.)

68

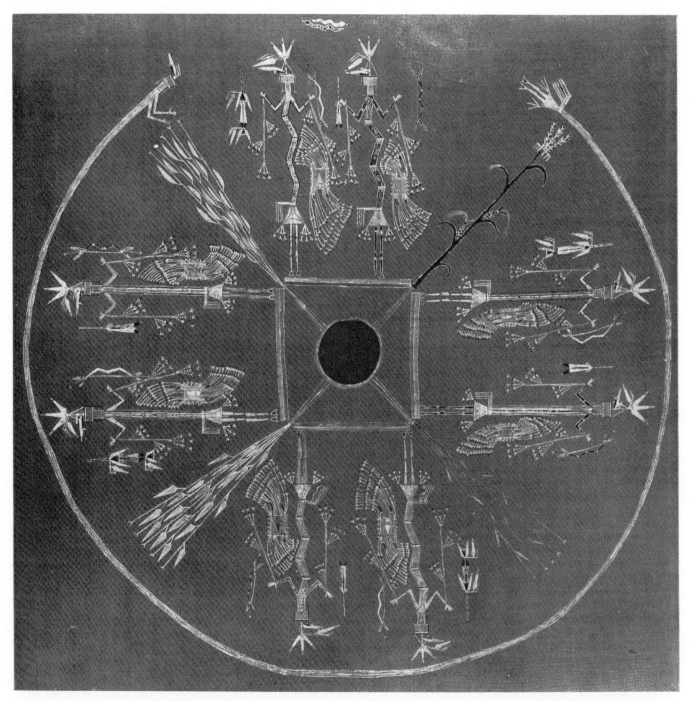

Plate 18.—Mixed Snake People, Male Shootingway. (No. 13, Walcott catalog; USNM 377451; BAE negative 2457–b–2.)

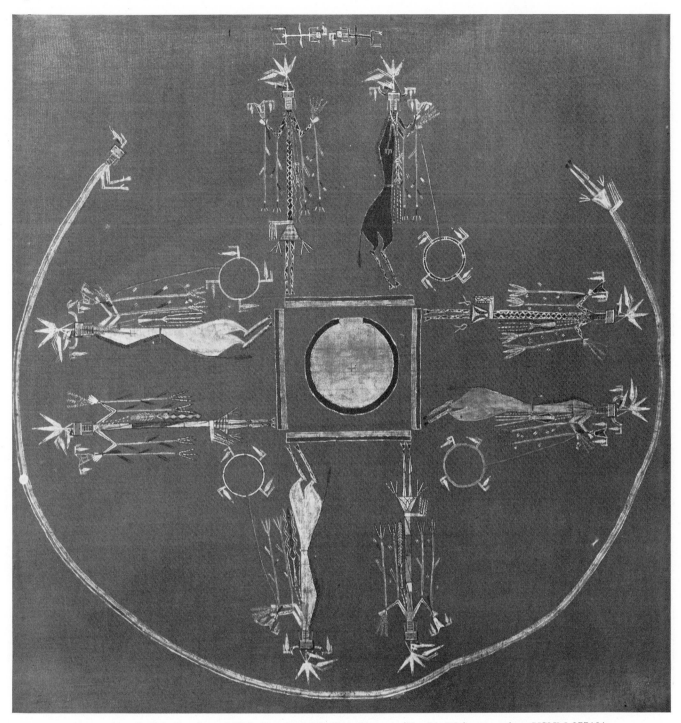

PLATE 19.—Buffalo People and Holy People, Male Shootingway. (No. 14, Walcott catalog; USNM 377464; BAE negative 2457–b–15.)

PLATE 20.—Buffalo and homes, Male Shootingway. (No. 15, Walcott catalog; USNM 377469; BAE negative 2457–b–20.)

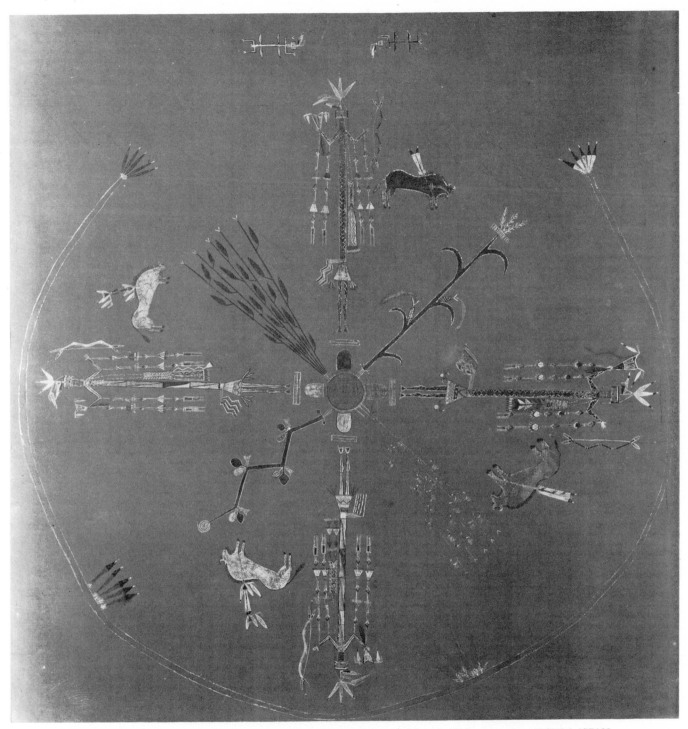

PLATE 21.—Holy People Overcome Buffalo, Male Shootingway. (No. 16, Walcott catalog; USNM 377463; BAE negative 2457–b–14.)

72

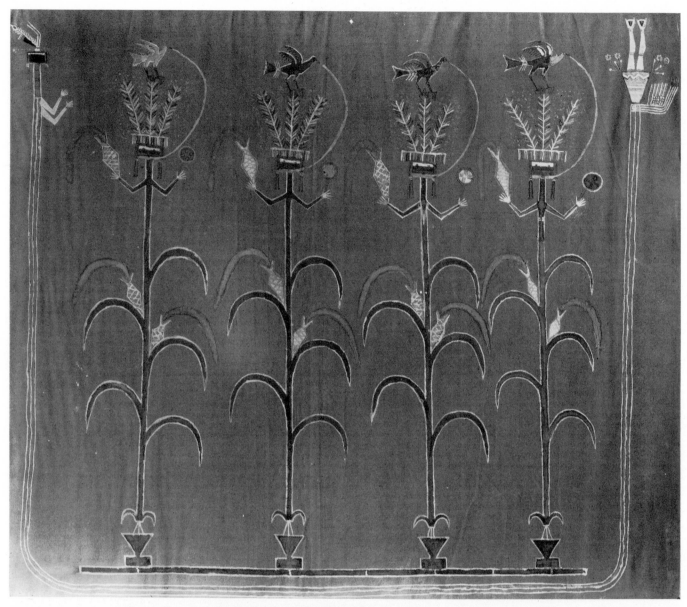

PLATE 22.—Corn People, Male Shootingway. (No. 17, Walcott catalog; USNM 377459;
BAE negative 2457–b–10.)

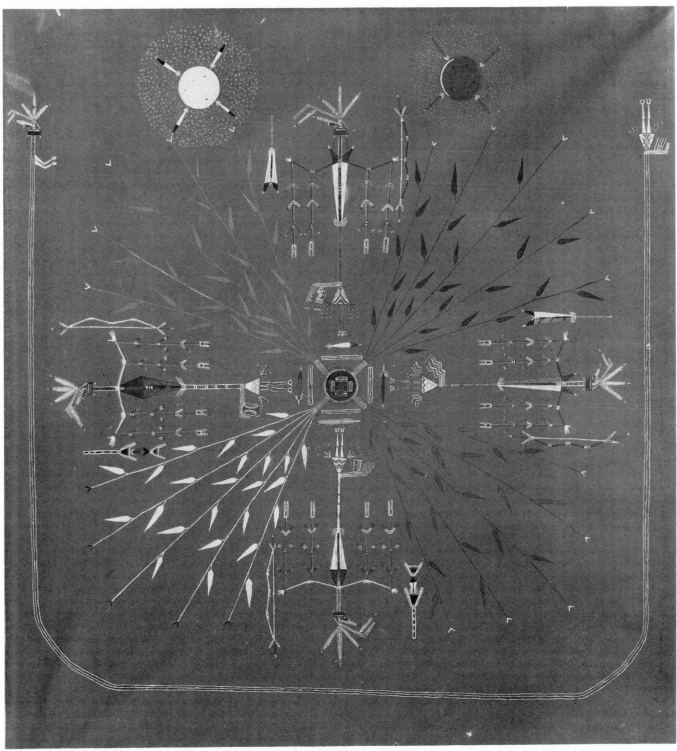

PLATE 23.—Tail-feathered Arrow People, Male Shootingway. (No. 18, Walcott catalog; USNM 377468; BAE negative 2457–b–19.)

PLATE 24.—Dancers with Sun, Moon, and Winds, Mountain-Shootingway. (No. 19, Walcott catalog; USNM 377470; BAE negative 2457–b–21.)

PLATE 25.—Dancers with Sun, Moon, and Wind symbols, wearing Shootingway headdresses. Photograph taken about 1935 at the Intertribal Indian Ceremonial, Gallup, New Mexico.

PLATE 26.—Dancers with Sun, Moon, and Wind Wands, Mountain-Shootingway. (No. 20, Walcott catalog;
USNM 377457, right half; BAE negative 2457–b–8, right half.)

PLATE 27.—Dancers carrying Sun, Moon, and Wind Wands. Photograph taken about 1935 at the Intertribal Indian Ceremonial, Gallup, New Mexico.

78

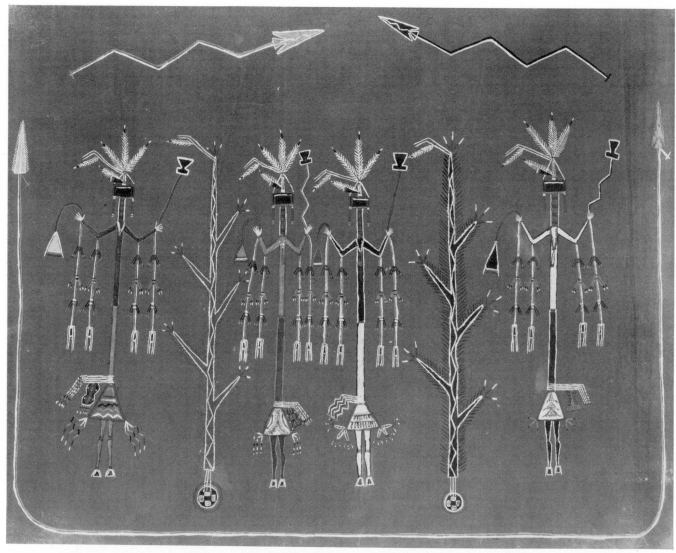

PLATE 28.—Dancers with Cactus, Mountain-Shootingway. (No. 21, Walcott catalog; USNM 377458; BAE negative 2457–b–9.)

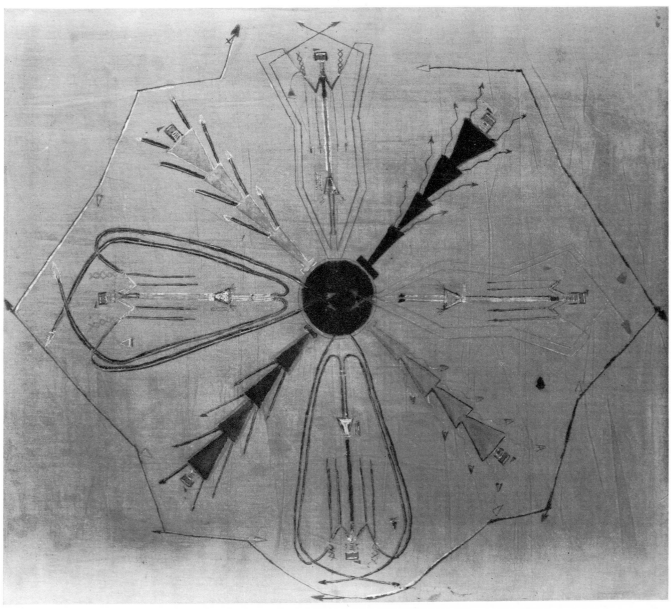

PLATE 29.—Dancers with Lightnings, Mountain-Shootingway. (No. 22, Walcott catalog; USNM 377456; BAE negative 2457–b–7.)

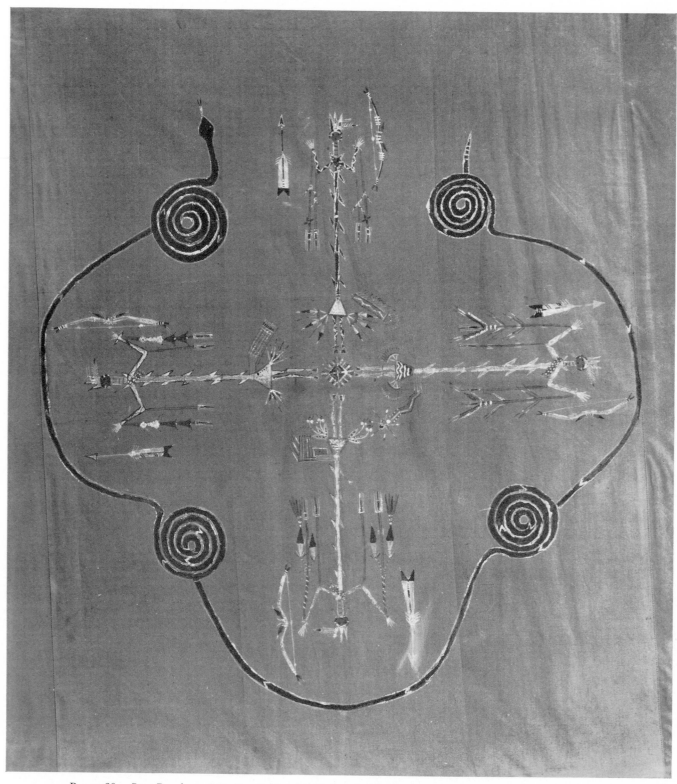

PLATE 30.—Star People and Endless Snake, Big Starway. (No. 23, Walcott catalog; USNM 377461; BAE negative 2457–b–12.)

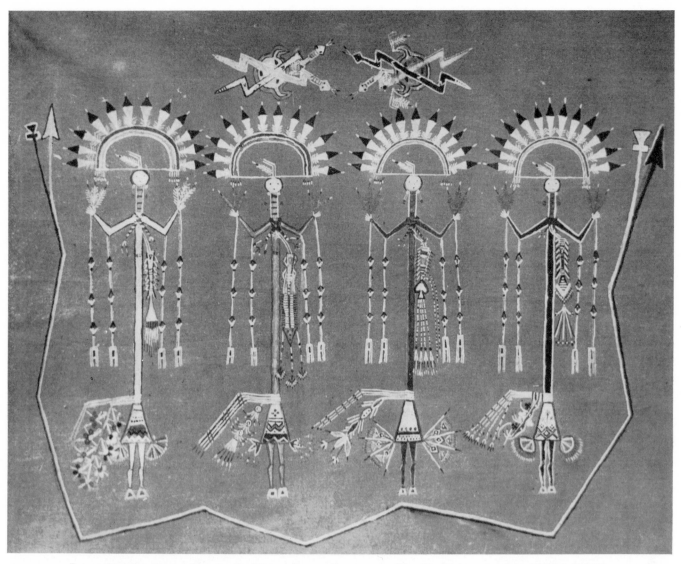

PLATE 31.—Beautyway Dancers in Mountainway, Beautyway. (No. 24, Walcott catalog; USNM 377457, left half; BAE negative 2457–b–8, left half.)

82

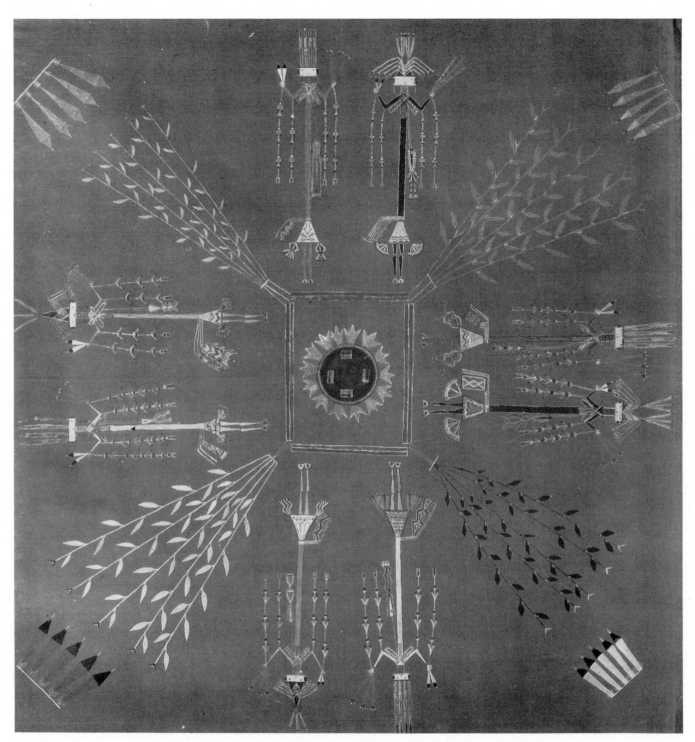

PLATE 32.—People of the Myth, Beautyway (No. 25, Walcott catalog; USNM 377471; BAE negative 2457–b–22).

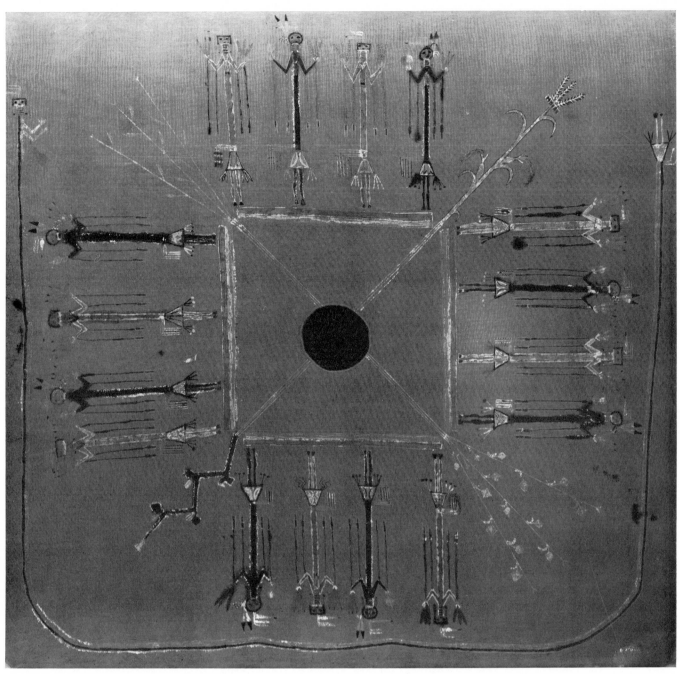

PLATE 33.—First Dancers, Nightway. (No. 26, Walcott catalog; USNM 377454; BAE negative 2457–b–5.)

84

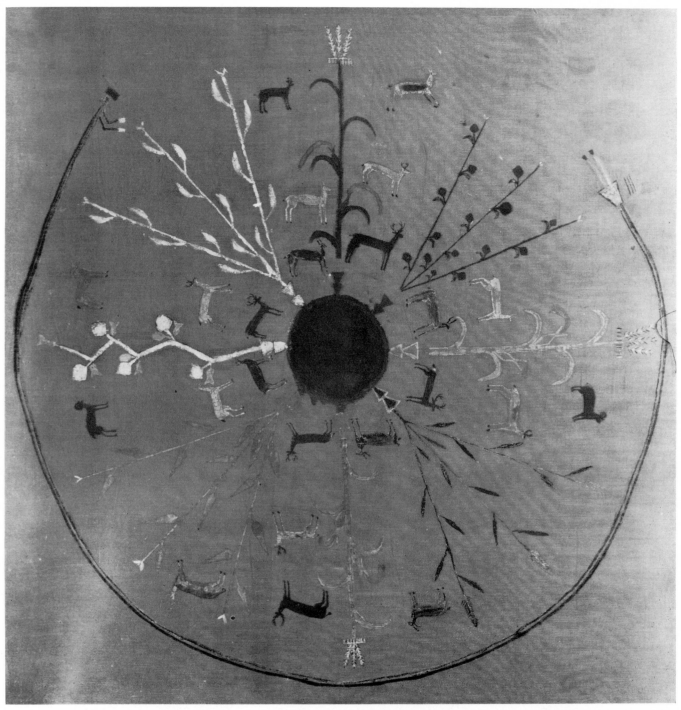

PLATE 34.—The Farm, Plumeway. (No. 27, Walcott catalog; USNM 377466; BAE negative 2457–b–17.)

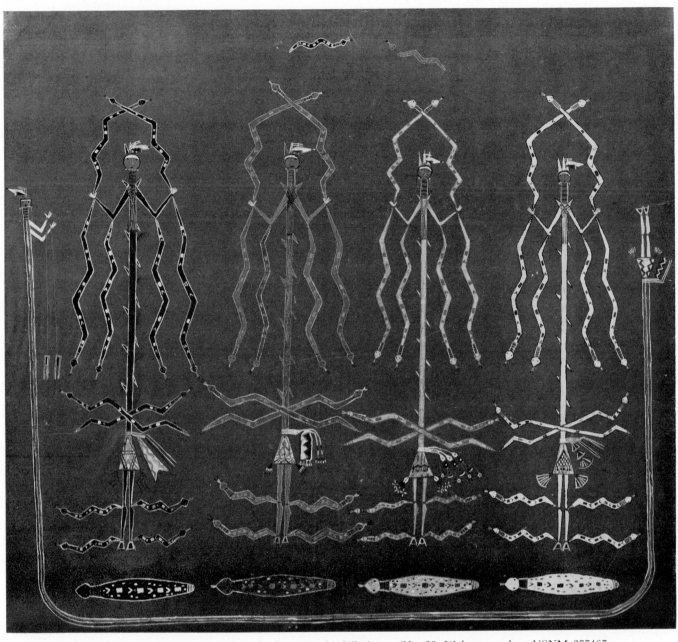

PLATE 35.—Wind People dressed in Snakes, Navaho Windway. (No. 28, Walcott catalog; USNM 377467; BAE negative 2457–b–18.)

86

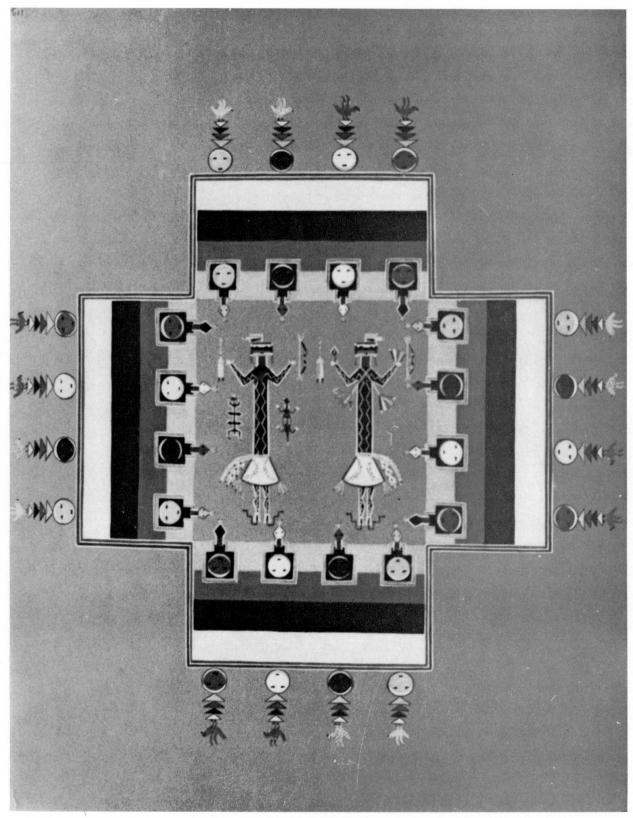

PLATE 36.—Sun's Houses with Slayer Twins, Male Shootingway; recorded by Franc J. Newcomb before 1937.
(Courtesy Columbia University.)

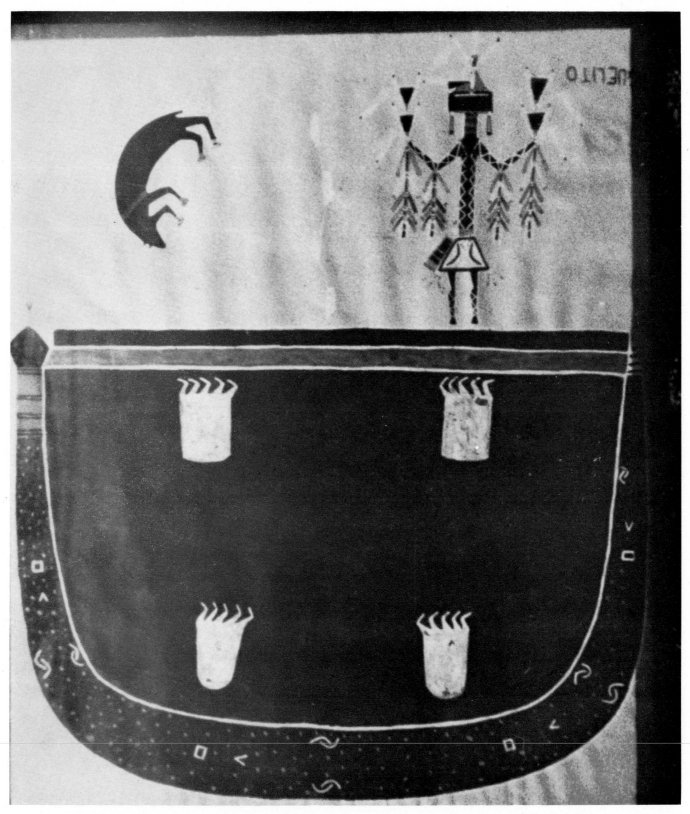

PLATE 37.—Big Snake with Holy Young Man and the Bear, Shock rite sandpainting, Male Shootingway, by Red Point (Miguelito), near Ganado, Arizona; collected by Ramon Hubbell about 1930. (Courtesy Museum of Navaho Ceremonial Art.)

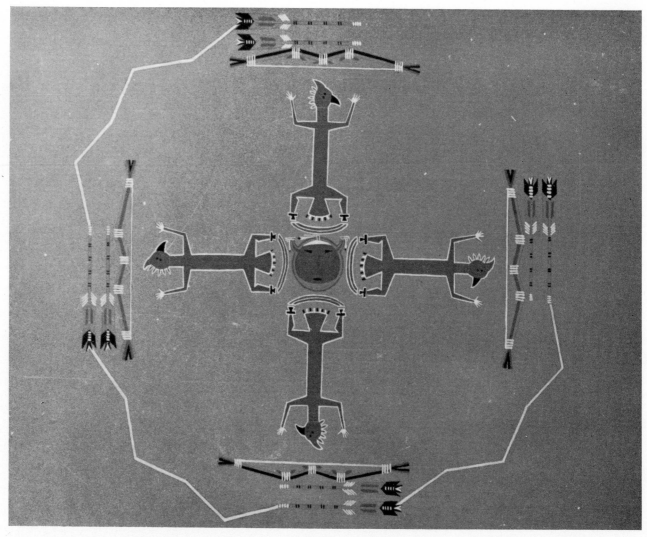

PLATE 38.—Kingbird (Titmouse) People, Female Shootingway, by Hastin Begay, Chinle, Arizona, collected by Mary C. Wheelwright in 1947. (Courtesy Museum of Navaho Ceremonial Art.)

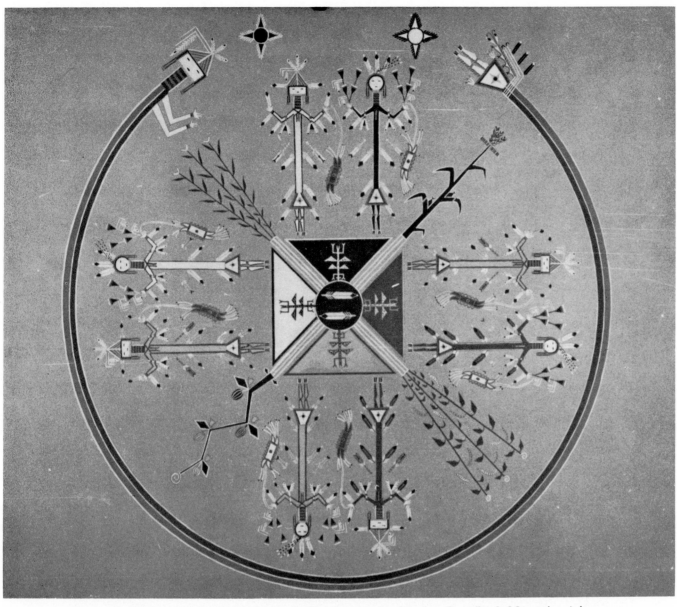

PLATE 39.—White Nostril People, Mountain-Shootingway by Massive One, Black Mountain, Arizona; collected by Laura A. Armer in 1929. (Courtesy Museum of Navaho Ceremonial Art.)

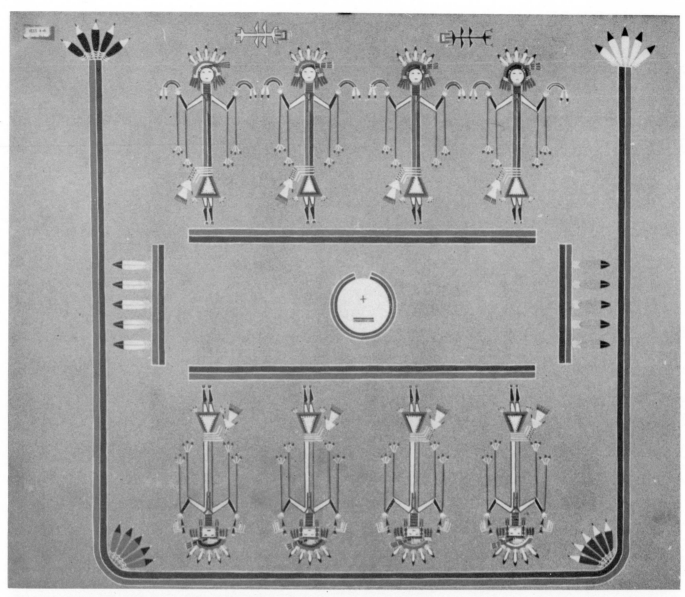

PLATE 40.—Mountain Sheep People at the Rock Rim, Mountain-Shootingway, by Massive One, Black Mountain, Arizona; collected by Laura A. Armer in 1929. (Courtesy Museum of Navaho Ceremonial Art.)

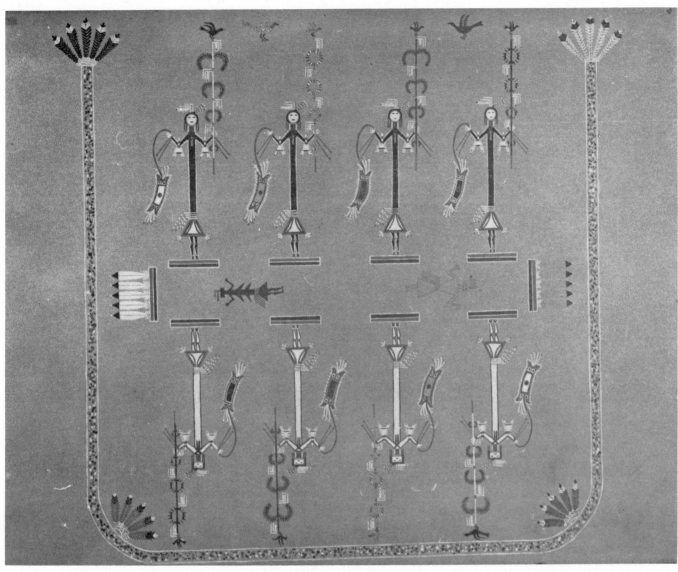

PLATE 41.—Mountain Sheep People carrying poles, Mountain-Shootingway, by Massive One, Black Mountain, Arizona; collected by Laura A. Armer in 1929. (Courtesy Museum of Navaho Ceremonial Art.)

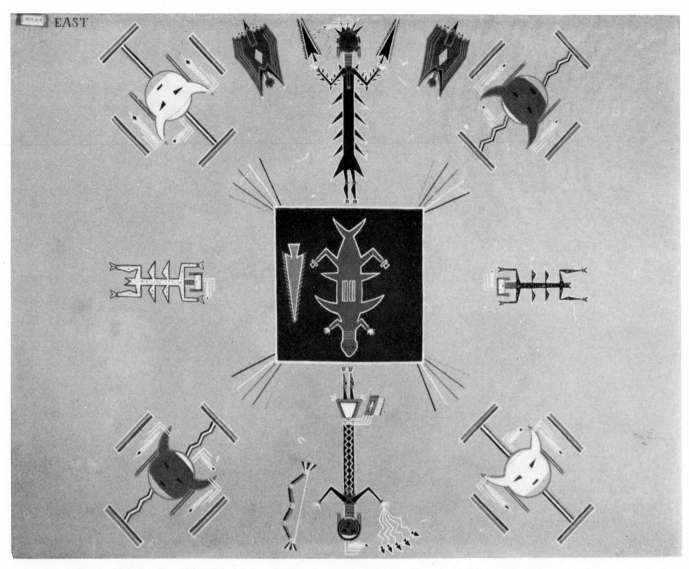

PLATE 42.—Swallowed by Fish, Mountain-Shootingway by Massive One, Black Mountain, Arizona; collected by Laura A. Armer in 1929. (Courtesy Museum of Navaho Ceremonial Art.)

PLATE 43.—Moon clothed in Snakes with Born-for-Water, Mountain-Shootingway, Sam Tilden, Canyon de Chelly, Arizona; collected by Bertha Dutton in 1940. (Courtesy Museum of New Mexico.)

94

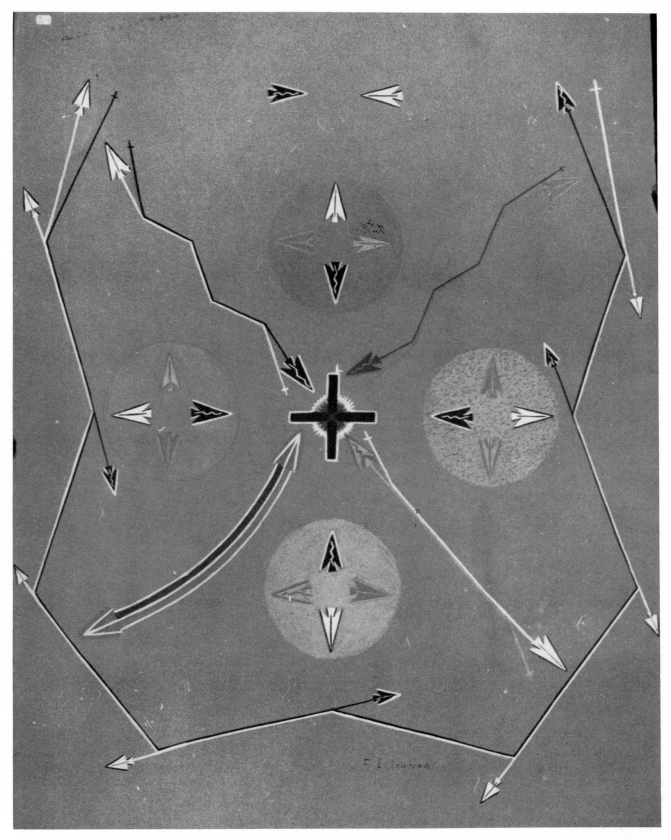

PLATE 44.—Baskets of Arrows, Male Shootingway Evilway; recorded by Franc J. Newcomb before 1933.
(Courtesy Museum of Navaho Ceremonial Art.)

Index

361–838 O—70——9